Cheng & Tsui Publications of Related Interest

HyperChinese CD ROMs (Macintosh)		
by Jing-heng Ma and Robert H. Smitheram	Grammar Modules	0-88727-193-6
	Pronunciation Modules	0-88727-223-1
Practical Chinese Reader		
Beijing Language Institute, Et. al.	Book 1-Traditional	0-88727-229-0
	Book 2-Traditional	0-88727-231-2
by Ziqiang Shr	Book 1-Video tape	0-88727-162-6
	Book 2-Video tape	0-88727-163-4
by Shou-hsin Teng	Writing Workbook (1&2)	0-88727-191-X
Chinese Unmasked		
by Jing-heng Ma	Textbook-Traditional	0-88727-190-1
	Textbook-Simplified	0-88727-198-7
Liuxue Shiyong Kouyu: Studying in China		
by Vivian Ling and James E. Dew	Textbook	0-88727-196-0
	Audio Cassettes	0-88727-197-9
Short Chinese TV Plays: An Intermediate Course		
by Shou-hsin Teng and Liu Yuehua	Paperback	0-88727-168-5
	2 Video Tapes	0-88727-169-3
Taiwan Today, 2nd Edition		
by Shou-hsin Teng and Lo Sun Perry	Paperback	0-88727-246-0
A Chinese Text for a Changing China		
by Irene Liu and Li Xiaoqi	Textbook	0-88727-232-0
	Audio Cassettes	0-88727-207-X
Chinese Breakthrough: Learning Chinese through TV and Newspapers		
by Hong Gang Jin, De Bao Xu, and John Berninghausen	Textbook	0-88727-194-4
	Audio Cassettes	0-88727-211-8
	Video tape	0-88727-195-2
	CD-ROM	0-88727-248-7
Beyond The Basics		
by Jianhua Bai, Juyu Sung, and Janet Xhiqun Xing	Textbook	0-88727-226-6
	Audio Cassettes	0-88727-250-9
Read Chinese Signs		
by Cornelius C. Kubler and Hsiaojung Sharon L. Chi	Institutional Edition	0-88727-182-0
	Private Edition	0-88727-183-9

Practical Chinese Reader Companion

Lessons 21-35 Traditional Character Edition Volume B

實用漢語學習手冊

Practical Chinese Reader Companion

Lessons 21-35 Traditional Character Edition Volume B

實用漢語學習手冊

Yihua Wang

Cheng & Tsui Company

About the Author

Yihua Wang has been a foreign language educator for over twenty years. She is presently a member of the faculty of the Modern Chinese Language Program at the University of California at Los Angeles.

1996 Printing

Practical Chinese Reader series textbooks, writing workbooks, computer software, video tapes, and audio tapes are available from the publisher.

Cheng & Tsui Company
25 West Street
Boston, MA 02111-1268 USA
Fax: (617) 426-3669

Library of Congress Catalog Card Number: 96-085884

Practical Chinese Reader Companion, Volume B
Traditional Character Edition ISBN: 0-88727-253-3
Simplified Character Edition ISBN: 0-88727-254-1

Printed in the United States of America

PUBLISHER'S NOTE

The Cheng & Tsui Company is pleased to announce the most recent additions to its Asian Language Series, **Practical Chinese Reader Companion**. This series of workbooks supplements the highly successful introductory Chinese language textbooks, **Practical Chinese Reader, Books I and II**. Designed for beginning students of Mandarin Chinese, the **Practical Chinese Reader** series emphasizes spoken competence through grammar explanations, supplementary reading materials, homework sheets, and other related references.

The **C&T Asian Language Series** is designed to publish and widely distribute quality language texts as they are completed by such leading institutions as the Beijing Language Institute, as well as other significant works in the field of Asian languages developed in the United States and elsewhere.

We welcome readers' comments and suggestions concerning the publications in this series. Please contact the following members of the Editorial Board:

INTRODUCTION

Practical Chinese Reader Companion, **Volumes A, B, and C** is a series designed to supplement the Beijing Language Institute's **Practical Chinese Reader, Books I and II** (or **PCR I and II**), one of the most widely used elementary Chinese text books at the college level in the United States and elsewhere. All three volumes in the **PCR Companion** series have been used with success for over six years by approximately 1400 students at the University of California, Los Angeles (UCLA).

Because of different school schedules and programs, it is sometimes difficult for schools to finish both **PCR I and II** in a single academic year. **PCR Companion**, therefore, is divided into three volumes to allow for more flexibility and is arranged to correspond with the lessons in **PCR I and II** in the following manner:

PCR Companion	PCR I and II
Volume A	Lessons 1 - 20
Volume B	Lessons 21 - 35
Volume C	Lessons 36 - 50

PCR Companion is available in both a simplified character edition and a traditional character edition. Each volume consists of three parts:

1) **Lecture Notes** help students to preview and review new grammar points introduced in each lesson. Explanations are written with special attention to comparisons between English and Chinese grammar, highlighting common errors made by English-speaking learners. Each presentation of a new sentence pattern is followed by illustrative sentences or mini-dialogs which help students to better understand the pattern and thus enable them to generate their own sentences accurately. In many chapters, interesting supplementary reading texts and exercises are provided to reinforce the new language points presented. In addition to grammar rules, socio-cultural rules are introduced when relevant. Situational dialogs --such as making phone calls, asking for directions, etc.-- are designed for some lessons to provide useful expressions needed in particular circumstances. In order to facilitate teaching and learning, the texts, lists of new words, and lists of characters in some lessons have been edited or replaced by new ones, and the order of presentation of some grammar points have been rearranged. For example, words in **PCR I and II** that are rarely used at the elementary level have been replaced by new, frequently-used words, such as *computer* and *freeway*. Characters newly introduced in each lesson are shown in an enlarged format to ensure that each stroke in the characters is clearly distinguishable.

2) **Homework** is included for every lesson and is designed to test the students' understanding of the language points introduced. Since homework pages in this book are perforated, instructors can ask students to tear out the pages to hand in for evaluation.

3) **Appendices** provide students with some useful references. *Appendix A* contains the texts in traditional characters for the corresponding lessons in **PCR I and II**. These are provided for students who wish to learn to read in traditional characters. *Appendix B* contains the answer key to the corresponding exercises in **PCR I and II**. *Appendix C*, which is found in **Volume C**, contains a glossary index of an edited vocabulary list covering *all* the lessons in **PCR I and II**.

For their insightful comments on the drafts of these books, my thanks go to Eileen Cheng, Xincun Huang, Steve Riep, Hong Zeng, and Ruey-jiuan Wu, who served as Teaching Assistants for the elementary Chinese courses at UCLA. Thanks are also owed to Professor Alan Lamson and the production staff at Cheng & Tsui for their excellent proofreading.

Comments and suggestions are welcomed.

August, 1996

Yihua Wang
wang@ucla.edu
Deptartment of East Asian Languages
UCLA
405 Hilgard Avenue
Los Angeles, CA 90095

CONTENTS

PART I. LECTURE NOTES

PART I

LECTURE NOTES

LESSON 21

GRAMMAR NOTES

1. Verb /Verb Phrase and Subject-Predicate Construction Modifying a Noun

When a noun is modified by a verb/verb phrase or a Sub.-Pred. construction, the structural particle 的 must be placed before the noun.

Verb Verb phrase Sub.-Pred.	的	Noun

Examples:

Modifier:	
Verb	學習的時候
	工作的地方 (dìfang, place)
Verb with an object	參加舞會的人
	去中國的那個學生
Verb with two objects	教我漢語的老師
	送她花兒的人
Verb phrases in series	去中國學漢語的那個學生
Pivotal structure	請我參加晚會的那個同學
Sub.-Pred. construction	他送的禮物
	我認識的漢字
	我們上課的那個教室
	我學習漢語的時候

Exercise: Give definitions for the following words by filling the blanks.

1) 咖啡館 ________________________ 的地方。

2) 圖書館 ________________________ 的地方。

3) 教室 ________________________ 的地方。

4) 書店 ________________________ 的地方。

5) 學生宿舍 ______________________ 的地方。

6) 電影院 _______________________ 的地方。

7) 漢語老師 _____________________ 的老師。

8) 圖書館員 _____________________ 的人。

9) 服務員 _______________________ 的人。

10) 德語 ________________________ 的話(huà, speech, language)。

2. The Modal Particle 吧

1) 吧 is often placed at the end of an imperative sentence (a request, command, advice, etc.) to soften the tone. It can also indicate agreement or approval.

A: 晚上我們去看一個電影吧 。

B: 好吧！看幾點的？

A: 十點的。

B: 十點太晚了，看七點的吧 。

2) 吧 is added to the end of a declarative sentence to indicate estimation. It can also turn a declarative sentence into an interrogative sentence, indicating that the speaker is not certain about what he thinks.

A: 那是她男朋友吧？

B: 不是吧。那個人很像她，是她哥哥吧。

A: 你知道她家的地址吧?

B: 知道 。

3. Reduplicated Verbs

1) Reduplicated verbs are used to express short and informal actions.

今天星期五，晚上我想在家休息休息 —

聽聽音樂， 看看電視 (diànshì, T.V.)， 寫寫信。

2) They are also used to soften the tone of imperative sentences.

A: 哪本雜誌好 ？ 請你給我介紹介紹 。

B: 這本很有意思，你看看吧。

NOTES:

1) Only action verbs can be reduplicated. Verbs such as 有, 在, 是 cannot be reduplicated.
2) 一 is often inserted between a monosyllabic verb and its reduplication.

   坐一坐 = 坐坐
   等一等 = 等等
3) The reduplicated verb can be replaced by 一下兒 .

   休息休息 = 休息一下兒
   跳跳舞 = 跳一下兒舞
4) The reduplicated verb, 一 and 一下兒 are not stressed in speech.
5) The reduplication pattern for disyllabic verbs is: <u>AB</u> <u>AB</u>

   學習學習 * xx 學學習習 xx
   參加參加 xx 參參加加 xx

4. Review of the Adjectival Predicate

1) Do not add 是 before the adjectival predicate.

   她很高興。 xx 她是很高興。 xx

2) When the adjectival predicate is not preceded by other adverbs, it should be modified by the adverb 很, which in this case does **not** indicate degree in meaning. Only when contrast/comparison is intended, 很 can be omitted.

- 這條裙子長， 那條裙子短 (duǎn, short)。
- 我有兩輛車, 一輛新， 一輛舊 。

3) Adverbs of degree are often used before the adjectival predicate.

真	(zhēn, really, truly)	真好, 真多
非常	(fēicháng, extremely)	非常高興, 非常年輕
太	(tài, too)	太舊, 太忙
更	(gèng, even , more)	更漂亮， 更有意思

4) When there is an adverb such as 常，也，不, 真 ，非常, 太, 更, before the adjectival predicate, the "Adj /V not Adj /V?" question cannot be formed.

   xx 她非常年輕不年輕? xx

   xx 你也去不去? xx

* Sentences or phrases marked with XX are ungrammatical.

In this case, other question forms are used instead:

- 她非常年輕嗎？
- 你也去，對嗎？

5. Asking a Person's Age

1) When asking a child or a person of your generation about his age:

- 你（今年）多大？

2) When asking a senior, a person older than yourself, or a person higher in social status than yourself about his age:

- 您（今年）多大歲數?

LEARN CHARACTERS

高 興(兴)、漂、亮、 輕(轻)、真、
gāo xìng piào liàng qīng zhēn

吧、非、送、跳、舞、 像(象)、更
ba fēi sòng tiào wǔ xiàng gèng

開(开)、門(门)、
kāi mén

*輛(辆)、休、息、時(时)、候、
liàng xiū xī shí hòu

地、方
dì fāng

Note: 1. Characters listed in the row marked with * are not listed in this lesson in PCR.
2. When a character has a simplified version, it is listed in the parentheses.

LESSON 22

GRAMMAR NOTES

l. Position Words

Position words are nouns showing spacial positions. In this lesson eleven position words are introduced:

上邊	shàngbiān	up, above, on, top
下邊	xiàbiān	below, under, bottom
左邊	zuǒbiān	left-hand side, on the left
右邊	yòubiān	right-hand side, on the right
裏邊	lǐbiān	inside
外邊	wàibiān	outside
前邊	qiánbiān	in front of, the front, before
後邊	hòubiān	at the back of, the back, behind
旁邊	pángbiān	at the side of, side
中間	zhōngjiān	between, the middle, the center
對面	duìmiàn	opposite

l) When a position word is modified by another noun, the structural particle 的 is optional, but when a position word is modifying another noun, 的 is mandatory.

NOUN (的) + POSITION

車（的）外邊　　outside the car
臥室（的）中間　　in the middle of the bedroom
桌子（的）前邊　　in front of the desk

POSITION + 的 + NOUN

外邊的車	the car outside
中間的臥室	the bedroom in the middle
前邊的桌子	the desk in the front

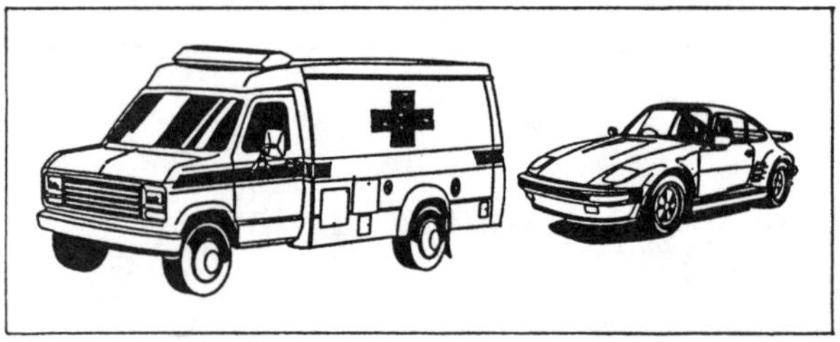

前邊的車大，後邊的車小。
大車後邊的車是我的。
我的車前邊的車是醫院的。

2) When 上邊，裏邊 and 外邊 are modified by other nouns, 邊 is often omitted, e.g. 客廳**裏**， 圖書館**裏**
桌子上， 報上
國外， 城外

3) Do not use 裏邊 in the following cases:

a. after geographical terms

- 加州有很多大學。 XX 加州裏邊有很多大學。 XX

b. in the phrase of " 在 + place / organization / building "

- 他在北京大學工作。 XX 他在北京大學裏邊工作。 XX

2. Sentence Patterns Showing Existence

1) There is something at this place.

POSITION + 有+ NOUN (indefinite)

A: 後邊有甚麼?
What's there in the back?

B: 後邊有一個車房 。
There is a garage in the back.

2) Certain thing exists at this place.

NOUN (definite) + 在 + POSITION

A: 花園在哪兒？
Where is the garden?

B: 花園在車房（的）右邊。
The garden is to the right of the garage.

3) It is known that there is something at this place or a certain thing exists at this place. Now identify what it is.

POSITION + 是 + NOUN (def./indef.)

A: 車房（的）前邊是甚麼？
B: 車房（的）前邊是一輛大車。

王家的車房

車房旁邊有一個小花園。
車房裏邊和外邊都有車。
車房裏的車是王太太的。
王先生的車在車房外邊。
前邊的車不是王家的， 是郵局的。

LEARN CHARACTERS

邊(边)、左、 裏(里)、旁、厨、房、
biān zuǒ lǐ páng chú fáng

間(间)、面、餐、 廳(厅)、臥、
jiān miàn cān tīng wò

園(园)、桌、椅、洗、澡、 幫(帮)
yuán zhuō yǐ xǐ zǎo bāng

* 右、把
yòu bǎ

READING EXERCISE

丁雲的宿舍

丁雲在留學生宿舍住。她住二層二六一號 。她的房間不大，門的左邊有一個大窗戶。 窗戶前邊是一張書桌。書桌前邊有兩把椅子; 書桌上有一台 (tái, measure word)電腦 (diànnǎo, computer)。書桌旁邊是一個大書架 (shūjià, bookshelf), 書架上有很多書 。丁雲的床在書桌對面, 床右邊的小桌子上有一個電視機 (diànshìjī, TV set)。牆 (qiáng, wall)上有一張中國地圖和一張丁雲爸爸媽媽的照片。丁雲常常整理她的房間。她的房間總是很整齊(zhěngqí, neat)。

EXERCISE Describe the following pictures.

1.

2.

3.

4.

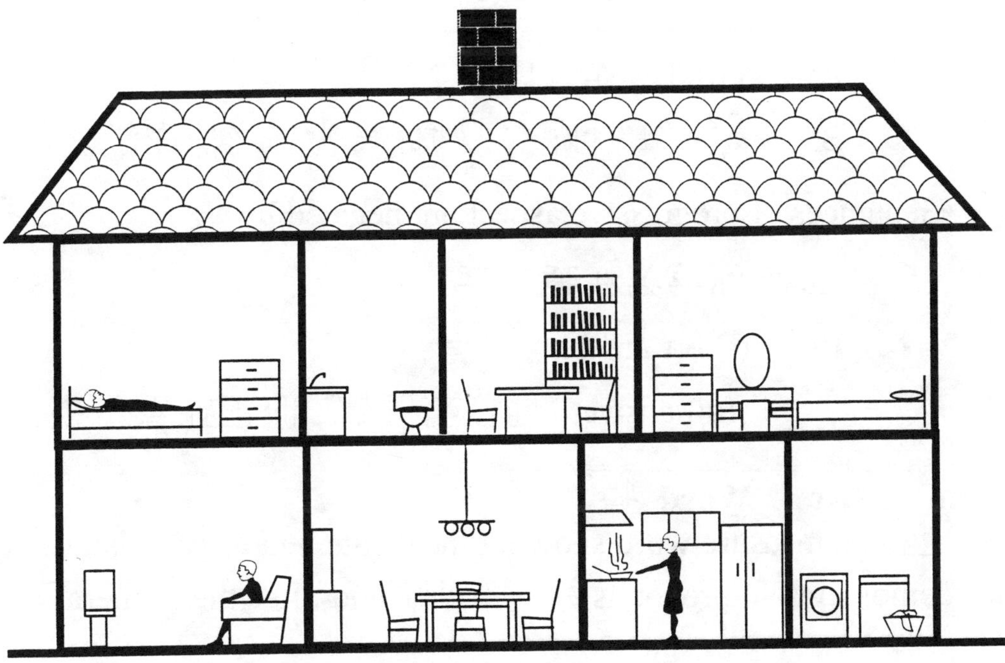

LESSON 23

GRAMMAR NOTES

1. The Progressive Aspect

There are no tenses in Chinese. Since Chinese verbs don't conjugate, the **time** of an event (past, present and future) is shown by time words, such as 以前, 現在, 明天, etc. The **aspect** of an event (in progress, continuing, completed, etc.) is shown by aspect particles and adverbs.

The progressive aspect indicates an event is in progress. It is expressed by the following two patterns:

1.	正 正在 在	+ VERB (+ OBJECT) + (呢)

A: 你在作甚麼 ?

B: 我正聽新聞呢 。/我在看電視。 /我正在學中文。

2.	VERB (+ OBJECT) + 呢

A: 你同屋作甚麼呢 ?

B: 她打電話呢。/她休息呢。/她作飯呢 。

Sentences of progressive aspect are negated by 沒有:

A: 你弟弟在睡覺嗎?

B: (short answer) 沒有。

(full answer) 他沒有睡覺, 他正在看電視。

2. The Measure Word 些

些 is a measure word showing indefinite quantity. It is usually used after demonstrative pronouns 這, 那, 哪 and after the numeral 一 .

A:　那些 (those) 照片是誰的？

B:　哪些 (which ones)?

A:　桌子上的那些 (those)。

B:　一些 (some) 是我的，一些是我姐姐的。

些 can not be followed by numerals. To express the idea of "those five chairs", the phrase should be:

那五把椅子　　　　xx 那些五把椅子 xx

3. The Interrogative Pronoun 怎麼樣 (zěnmeyàng)

1) as a casual greeting between close friends:

A:　你怎麼樣？(How is it going?)

B:　很好, 你呢？

2) as a suggestion:

A:　我們明天去城外玩兒, 怎麼樣? (= 好不好?)

B:　好!

3) asking for opinions:

A:　我的新車怎麼樣？(How is my new car?)

B:　太好了!

4. Making Telephone Calls

1)　A:　喂?

B:　喂, 小丁在嗎？

A:　這兒沒有小丁, 你打錯了。

(Nǐ dǎ cuò le, You dialed the wrong number.)

B:　對不起。

2)　A:　喂?

B:　喂, 我找小丁。

A:　我就是。你是小張吧?......

3)　B:　喂, 我找小丁。

A:　他不在。您貴姓？您有甚麼事兒?

B:　我姓張, 我的電話是(310) 206-8235。請他給我打一個電話。

4) A: 喂?
B: 喂, 小丁在嗎？
A: 在, 請等一等 。...... 小丁, 你的電話。

LEARN CHARACTERS

正 視(视)、接、話(话)、玩、打、
zhèng shì jiē huà wán dǎ

複(复)、聞 (闻)、廠 (厂)、出、發(发)、
fù wén chǎng chū fā

訪 (访)、照、片、城、睡、覺(觉)
fǎng zhào piàn chéng shuì jiào

* 些、怎、樣(样)
xiē zěn yàng

EXERCISE Describe the following picture, using the progressive aspect.

LESSON 25

GRAMMAR NOTES

1. The Complement of Degree

A predicate verb (or a predicate adjective) is sometimes followed by a word or a phrase to further explain or complete its meaning. This word or phrase is a **complement**.

A complement which shows the degree or extent of an action, or the degree or extent of a state is a **complement of degree**.

A: 他學習得怎麼樣?
B: 他學習得很好。
A: 他工作得怎麼樣 ?
B: 他工作得也很好。

The sentence patterns of the simple complement of degree are as follows:

1. without obj	V + 得 + Adj

- 他學得很快。

2. with obj	V + O + V + 得 + Adj

- 他學中文學得很快。

3. with preposed obj	O + V+ 得 + Adj

- 他中文學得很快。/中文他學得很快。

Insert 不 before the adjective to make the negative form:

4. ...... 得 + 不 + Adj

- 他歌唱得好, 舞跳得不好。
- 我游泳游得不快 , 你呢 ?

The interrogative forms are as follows:

5.	......	得 Adj 不 Adj ?	
6.	......	得 怎麼樣?	
7.	......	得 Adj 嗎?	

- 你開車開得好不好?
- 你開車開得怎麼樣?
- 你開車開得好嗎?

Since the concept of the complement of degree in Chinese has no counterpart in the English language, what is expressed by the complement of degree in Chinese is expressed in English by the use of an adverb. Because of the complement of degree, the Chinese language can make a finer distinction than English in expressing **the pure manner of an action** (by an adverb) **and the result of an action** (by a complement of degree). For example:

Manner	**Result**
- 他常常寫漢字。	- 他漢字寫得很漂亮。
- 他非常喜歡跳舞 。	- 他跳舞跳得很高興 。

The complement of degree cannot be used with verbs such as 有, 在, 是 , because these verbs do not indicate actions and hence cannot express the degree.

xx 他有中國朋友有得很多。 xx
xx 他在圖書館在得很多 。 xx

The correct sentences should be:
- 他有很多中國朋友 。
- 他常常在圖書館。

2. The Preposed Object

The regular sentence order in Chinese is S-V-O, but in the following cases the object is often preposed before the verb, and either before or after the subject.

S - O -V
O - S - V

1) when the object is long or complicated -

- 那位中國老師說的話我不懂。

- 我昨天買的那本書他正在看呢 。
- 王老師旁邊的那個人你認識嗎 ？

2) when comparison or emphasis is intended -

- 他日本飯作得好，中國飯作得不好 。
- 這個字我不認識，那個字我也不認識。

LEARN CHARACTERS

得、	停、	河、	游、	泳、	快、	慢、	錯(错)、
de	tíng	hé	yóu	yǒng	kuài	màn	cuò

準(准)、	備(备)、	魚(鱼)、	湯(汤)、	位、
zhǔn	bèi	yú	tāng	wèi

* 答、	難(难)、	練 (练)、	懂、	起、	床、	助
dá	nán	liàn	dǒng	qǐ	chuáng	zhù

EXERCISE Make sentences of complement of degree with the following verbs.

Monosyllabic			**Disyllabic**		**V-O structure**	
來	去	走	告訴	介紹	睡覺	洗澡
吃	喝	看	參觀	複習	唱歌	跳舞
聽	問	說	出發	休息	游泳	吸煙
給	買	送	訪問	歡迎	起床	
打	開	停	準備	認識		
回	寫	懂	幫助	回答		
要	想	玩	工作	學習		
			練習			

LESSON 26

GRAMMAR NOTES

l. Optative Verbs (auxiliary verbs)

Optative verbs are put before the main verbs to express wishes, intentions, possibility or ability. The seven most frequently used optative verbs, their negative forms and their functions are listed below:

<table>
<tr><th></th><th>1 要
yào</th><th>2 想
xiǎng</th><th>3 願意
yuànyì</th><th>4 能
néng</th><th>5 可以
kěyǐ</th><th>6 會
huì</th><th>7 應該
yīnggāi</th></tr>
<tr><td>subjective wish, desire or request</td><td>want
要
不要</td><td>would like to
想
不想</td><td>be willing to
願意
不願意</td><td></td><td></td><td></td><td></td></tr>
<tr><td>objective necessity</td><td>have to, ought to
要
*不用</td><td></td><td></td><td></td><td></td><td></td><td>should
應該
不應該</td></tr>
<tr><td>ability or skill acquired</td><td></td><td></td><td></td><td colspan="3">can, be able to
能 可以 會
不能 *不能 不會</td><td></td></tr>
<tr><td>ability depending on circumstances</td><td></td><td></td><td></td><td colspan="2">can, be able to
能 可以
不能 *不能</td><td></td><td></td></tr>
<tr><td>permission</td><td></td><td></td><td></td><td colspan="2">may, have permission to
能 可以
不能 不可以</td><td></td><td></td></tr>
<tr><td>probability, possibility</td><td></td><td></td><td></td><td></td><td></td><td colspan="2">be likely to, ought to, will probably
會 應該
不會 不應該</td></tr>
</table>

* Pay attention to these three negative forms.

Rules:

1) To negate a sentence with an optative verb, the negative adverb should be put before the optative verb.

Negative Adv. + Opt V + Main V

– 我不想研究文學。

xx 我想不研究文學。 xx

2) To make an affirmative-negative question, use the optative verb instead of the main verb.

Opt V + Negative Opt V + Main V ?

– 你會不會唱中國民歌?

xx 你會唱不唱中國民歌 ? xx

3) It is possible to use more than one optative verb before the main verb.

– 你是北京人，<u>應該會</u>唱京劇。

2. Conjunctions "雖然 (suīrán) ..., 可是(kěshì) / 但是 (dànshì) ..."

This is a pair of conjunctions which links two clauses. The statements of the two clauses are contradictory.

(S1) 雖然 (S1) ..., 可是/但是 (S2) ...

雖然 (although) can be placed both before or after the subject in the first clause, while 可是 / 但是 (but) can only be placed at the beginning of the following clause, before the subject of that clause. Sometimes one of the conjunctions can be omitted.

– 雖然我每天送她花兒，可是她不喜歡我。

When there is only one subject, it is not necessary to repeat the subject in both clauses:

– 他雖然會說中文, 可是不會寫漢字。

3. Conjunctions 還是 (háishì) **and** 或者 (huòzhě)

Both words mean "or" in English. 還是 is used in alternative questions or in subordinate clauses after verbs such as "告訴", "知道 ", etc. 或者 is used in statements and questions (except alternative questions).

1) A: 你喝茶還是咖啡 ?

B: 都不喝。你有橘子水或者牛奶嗎?

2) A: 你想去中國或者日本學習嗎？
B: 我想去中國。我想研究中國文學或者中國音樂。

3) A: 請告訴我 Lu Xun 是作家還是音樂家 ？
B: 我不知道他是作家還是音樂家 。
C: 你研究中國文學 ， 你應該知道他是作家還是音樂家 。

4) 爸爸: 你以後想作甚麼工作？
想當大夫還是當律師(lǜshī, lawyer)？

小張： 你總是問我想當大夫還是律師 ！
大夫或者律師我都不想當, 我想當老師 ！

4. Adverbs 才 and 就

才 and 就 are used before the main verb to indicate the speaker's subjective attitude as to whether the event expressed by the main verb is later than expected or earlier than expected.

1) - 我每天七點吃晚飯 。
- 小張五點就吃晚飯 。(as early as 5 o'clock, 太早了!)
- 小謝十點才吃晚飯。 (as late as 10 o'clock, 太晚了!)

2) - 小張四歲的時候就會游泳。 (How early!)
- 他爸爸今年才學游泳 。 (How late!)

3) 小張不是我的老朋友, 我今年才認識他。
他是小謝的老朋友，他們五年以前就認識 。

Word order: When there is a time expression in the sentence, 才 or 就 is placed <u>after</u> it. When there is an optative verb in the sentence, 才 or 就 should be placed <u>before</u> it.

Time Word + 才/ 就 + Optative Verb + Main Verb

我下午四點就能回家， 我哥哥七點才能回家 。
我今年就可以去中國， 我哥哥明年才能去。

LEARN CHARACTERS

談(谈)、	能、	可、	以、	會(会)、	研、	究、
tán	néng	kě	yǐ	huì	yán	jiū

容、	易、	應(应)、	該(该)、	或、	者、	就
róng	yì	yīng	gāi	huò	zhě	jiù

*	才、	雖(虽)、	然、	願(愿)、	當(当)
	cái	suī	rán	yuàn	dāng

但、	念、
dàn	niàn

EXERCISE

1. Underline the optative words and translate the dialogs into English.

1) A: 我以後想當老師，你呢？
   B: 我不想當老師，我要研究文學。

2) A: 我們每星期要學四十個漢字，太多了。
   B: 這星期不用學四十個。

3) A: 我能用中文寫信，你能嗎？
   B: 我雖然不會寫中文信，可是我可以看中文報。

4) A: 你可以跟我一起去游泳嗎？
   B: 不能，我有課。

5) A: 他下午會不會來？
   B: 我想他不會來，他今天有課。
   A: 可是他的課都是上午的，下午應該有空兒。

6) 星期六我不想去中文學校，我問媽媽：“我可以不去嗎？” 她說: “不可以。你是中國人，你應該會說中文，會寫漢字。”

2. Fill in the blanks with appropriate optative verbs.

1) A: 你 _____游泳嗎？

B: 我不_____。你 _____教我嗎？

2) A: 明天我去城外玩兒，_____不_____開你的車？

B: 對不起，明天我_____開車去工作，你不 _____開我的車。

3) A: 你 _____不_____告訴我他叫甚麼名字？

B: 你 _____知道他的名字，他是你妹妹的男朋友。

4) A: _____進來嗎？

B: 請進！

5) 閱覽室裏不_____唱歌，也不_____吃飯。

6) 老師，我明天上午有事兒，不_____來上漢語課。

7) A: 這兒_____ 不_____停車?

B: _____可以。

8) 我今年十六歲，還不_____喝酒呢。

READING EXERCISE

九點才起床

老師　九點上課，可是你總是九點半才來。你應該九點以前來教室。

小謝　可是我每天早上九點才起床。

老師　你睡覺睡得太多了！

小謝　雖然我起床起得很晚，可是睡得不多 - 我每天晚上在飯館工作，十二點才回家。

中國新年

小張　　二月十九號是中國新年，我們大學的中文老師和學中文的學生這星期五下午要開一個新年聯歡會 (liánhuān huì, party)。

小謝　　太好了！ 幾點開始？

小張　　三點半。歡迎你來參加。我們可以聽聽中國音樂，唱唱中國歌 ，跳跳中國舞，吃吃中國飯 。

小謝　　我一定去！ 我也要喝喝中國酒。中國的茅台(Máotái)酒很有名， 你們應該準備很多酒 。我要為你們的健康乾杯， 祝大家新年好！

小張　　謝謝你， 可是聯歡會上沒有酒 。

小謝　　沒有酒的聯歡會沒有意思， 我不想去！

LESSON 27

GRAMMAR NOTES

l. The Perfect Aspect with Particle 了

The aspect particle 了 is suffixed to a verb to emphasize that the action expressed by this verb is completed. The sentence patterns of perfect aspect are as follows:

1) affirmative	V 了
2) interrogative	V 了 沒有? V 了 嗎?
3) negative (了 is dropped)	沒（有）V 還沒（有）V 呢

A: 王老師來了沒有？
B: 她來了。
A: 張老師也來了嗎?
B: 他沒（有）來 。

l) The completion of an action has nothing to do with the time. A perfect aspect of an action can occur in the future:

A: (Before class) 你下了課去哪兒 ？
B: 我下了課去書店 。

A completed action often takes place in the past, but it doesn't mean all actions that take place in the past are in the perfect aspect:

- 以前他常常送我花兒 。
  (describing a habitual action in the past)

- 1990年我在日本學習, 1992 年我在英國學習。
  (stating the facts, not emphasizing the completion of 學習)

2) If the verb has an object, the object is usually modified:

- 我喝了兩瓶酒。
- 我喝了你送我的那瓶酒。

If the object is not modified, there is usually an adverbial modifier before the main verb, otherwise the sentence sounds incomplete.

- 我開車的時候喝了酒 。

If neither the object nor the verb is modified, the sentence sounds incomplete, a Chinese native speaker would wait for you to finish the sentence.

- 我喝了酒......

3) In a sentence with verbal constructions in a series, the perfect aspect marker 了 is usually suffixed to the second verb.

- 我用中文給我媽媽寫了一封信。
  v1 v2
- 我去中國城看了一個中國電影 。
  v1 v2

4) When the verb is reduplicated, the perfect aspect marker 了is placed before the reduplicated verb.

- 我試了試那條裙子, 真好看!

  xx 我試試了那條裙子。 xx
- 我嘗了嘗她作的菜，不好吃!

  xx 我嘗嘗了她作的菜 。 xx

2. Adverbs 又 (yòu), 還(hái) **and** 再 (zài)

The adverb "again" in English has three counterparts in Chinese - 又 , 還 and 再 . Although they all indicate the repetition of an action or a state, they are used in different situations.

1) 又 shows that the repetition of an action (or the repetition of the non-occurrence of an action) has already taken place.

A: 小張昨天來了, 今天他又來了嗎 ?

B: 又來了。 (The action "come 來" has been repeated.)

可是小王昨天沒有來，今天又沒有來。(The non-occurrence "didn't come 沒有來" has been repeated.)

又 can also indicate that the repetition of a periodic event or an action has not yet taken place, but one expects on the basis of past experience or natural law that the repetition will occur. In this case 又 is followed by 是 or an optative verb and the sentence ends with a 了.

- 明天又是星期五了，我又可以回家了, 又能吃媽媽作的飯了 。

2) 再 is used only in declarative sentences. It indicates that the repetition of an action or of a non-occurrence has **not** yet taken place, but will take place in the future.

- 今天我去的時候他不在家, 明天我再去。
- 小王昨天沒有來上課 ，今天又沒有來。 要是(if) 他明天再不來， 我們應該給他打一個電話 。

  (The non-occurrence 不來 is going to be repeated.)
- 那本小說沒有意思，我不想再看 。

  (When there is an optative verb in the sentence, 再 should be placed between the optative verb and the main verb.)

再 also indicates that an action was not repeated in the past. In this case it is placed after 沒有 and before the main verb:

- 我上個月給他寫了信以後 ，沒有再寫。

3) 還 is used in both interrogative and declarative sentences to express a repetition which is **not** yet realized, but will take place in the future.

A: 明天你還來嗎？

B: 還來。

還 can also be used in an interrogative or declarative sentence with an optative verb. It is placed **before** the optative verb, and an optional 再 can be placed after the optative verb.

A: 明天你還想（再）來嗎？

B: 還想（再）來。

We can now sum up the usage of these three adverbs as follows:

Repetition in the past:

又 V 了/ 又 V 了嗎 ？	did again, did again?
又沒（有） V	again did not do (non-occurrence repeated)
沒（有）再 V	did not do again (action not repeated)

Repetition in the future:

還 V 嗎 ? 還 opt v （再） V 嗎 ?	will do again? (will action be repeated?)
還 V / 再 V 還 opt v V/ opt v 再 V/ 還 opt v 再 V	will do again (action will be repeated)
不再 V/ 不 opt v 再 V 再不 V	will not do again (action will not be repeated) will not do again (non-occurrence will be repeated)

3. Action-Measure Words 次(cì) **and** 遍 (biàn)

1) Together with numerals, the action-measure words 次 and 遍 are placed after verbs as Action-Measure Complements (AMC) to show the frequency of actions.

numeral + 次 / 遍

- 昨天我給你打了五次電話 。

The word order of a sentence with action-measure complement is as follows:

1) without object S V AMC

- 你來了幾次 ?

2) with an object which is a pronoun S V O (pronoun) AMC

- 我找了她三次, 她都不在。
- 你想去那兒幾次 ?

3) with an object which is not a pronoun S V AMC O (non-pronoun)

- 我每星期上三次法語課 ， 五次漢語課 。

2) 遍 is different from 次 in that it emphasizes the whole process of an action from the beginning to the end.

A: 課文的錄音 (lù yīn, tape recording) 你聽了幾遍 ?

B: 我聽了一遍 。(the whole text - from the first line to the last line.)

A: 一遍太少 ，你應該聽三遍 。

A: 一遍太少 ，你應該聽三遍 。

LEARN CHARACTERS

又、再、為(为)、招、待、乾(干)、
yòu zài wèi zhāo dài gān

到、試(试)、始、健、嘗(尝)、康、
dào shì shǐ jiàn cháng kāng

菜、筷、化、樓(楼)
cài kuài huà lóu

* 次、遍
cì biàn

EXERCISE: Fill in the following blanks with adverbs 又/還/再 .

1. 古波想請帕蘭卡看電影。上個星期六 ，他給帕蘭卡打電話，帕蘭卡不在家 。這個星期五，古波 _____ 給她打電話，她 _____ 不在家 ，古波很不高興。他想：“明天我 _____ 打一次 ，要是帕蘭卡 _____ 不在，我請丁雲去看電影。”

星期六，帕蘭卡在家 。古波說: “我知道你喜歡看 ‘美*人和野獸* (yěshòu, beast)’，你 _____ 想 _____ 看一次嗎 ？”帕蘭卡說: “我 _____ 想看 。”

晚上 ，古波跟帕蘭卡到電影院的時候，那兒買票的人很多，帕蘭卡不願意等 ，她說: “今天看電影的人太多了。我們明天 _____ 來吧。” 古波說: “我們去看 ‘*獅子王* ’ (Shīzi Wáng, Lion King) 吧？” 帕蘭卡說: “那個電影我已經看過兩遍了 ，不想 _____ 看了。”

2. 明天 _____ 是星期六了，我 _____ 可以休息休息了。

3. 一九九二年我去了一次中國。
一九九三年我 _____ 去了一次 。
九三年以後我沒有 _____ 去。
明年我想 _____ 去一次 。

4. A: 這個電影真不錯 。我想 _____ 看一次 。你 _____ 想看嗎？
B: 我已經看了兩次了 。不想 _____ 看了。

5. A: 前天 (qiántiān, the day before yesterday) 我給他打了一個電話， 他不在家。昨天我 _____ 打了一次 ，他 _____ 不在家 。
B: 你今天 _____ 打了嗎?
A: 沒有 _____ 打。
B: 他很忙， 每天晚上九點才回家 。你今天晚上 _____ 打一次吧 。

6. A: 下學期你 _____ 要學中文嗎?
B: 我 _____ 想學。你呢？
A: 我不想 _____ 學了，我太忙了。

7. A: 你作的飯真好吃 ，我 _____ 想 _____ 吃一點兒 。
B: 對不起 ，沒有了。你明天 _____ 來吧， 我明天 _____ 給你作 。

8. 他昨天沒來上課 ，今天 _____ 沒來。明天他 _____ 不來，我們應該給他打一個電話 。

9. 我昨天買的這件襯衫真好看 。我 ____ 想 ____買一件 。

LESSON 28

GRAMMAR NOTES

l. The Modal Particle 了 (sentence-final了)

The modal particle了 occurs at the end of a sentence. It modifies the whole sentence, signifying that the event referred to has already taken place and is relevant to the present situation.

A: 小張在家嗎?

B: 不在, 他去看足球賽了。

(He went to watch a football game - and as a result, he is not home.)

The sentence patterns are as follows:

1) affirmative: S V O 了.	他看足球賽了。
2) interrogative: S V O 了沒有? S V O 了嗎?	他看足球賽了沒有? 他看足球賽了嗎?
3) negative: S 沒（有）V O.	他沒（有）看足球賽。

When there is no object in the sentence, the 了 at the end of the sentence functions both as the perfect aspect particle and the modal particle:

A: 日本隊贏了嗎?

B: 沒有贏, 輸了。

Since the action of a past event is often completed, both perfect aspect particle 了and modal particle 了 can be found in the same sentence:

A: 你買了帽子了嗎 ?

B: 我買了鞋了, 還沒買帽子呢 。

Attention: A simple statement about events that happened in the past does not require a 了 at the end of the sentence.

A: 你昨天在家嗎 ?

B: 我昨天上午去圖書館 ， 下午看球賽, 晚上沒出去 。

2. Sequential Actions

Both the following sentence patterns indicate that action 2 takes place immediately after action 1. Use pattern 1 when referring to events that happened in the past. Use pattern 2 when talking about future plans.

l) Both V1 and V2 took place in the past.

1. Vl 了(Ol), (就) V2 (O2)了

- 昨天我下了課（就）去看足球賽了。

2) Both V1 & V2 will take place in the future.

2. V1 了(O1), (就) V2 (O2)

- 今天我下了課（就）去看足球賽。

LEARN CHARACTERS

足、球、賽(赛)、隊(队)、帽、箱、
zú qiú sài duì mào xiāng

冰、鞋、冬、雙(双)、公、平、踢、
bīng xié dōng shuāng gōng píng tī

輸(输)、贏(赢)、比、滑
shū yíng bǐ huá

EXERCISE Insert 了 into the following sentences when necessary.

1. 明天我吃早飯去圖書館複習課文。
2. 去年夏天我常常去體育場看足球賽。
3. 我昨天晚上看老師給我們介紹的那本小說。
4. A: 王老師來嗎？

   B: 還沒來呢。他告訴我他下課就來。
5. A: 你聽今天早上的新聞沒有？

B: 沒聽，可是我看今天的報。我每天早上都看報才吃早飯 。

6. A: 昨天晚上我給你打電話的時候你不在家 。你去哪兒 ？

B: 我去看電影 。

7. 我昨天很想去參加你的生日舞會，可是我沒有空兒。

8. 以前我很喜歡聽日本音樂，常常買日本唱片。
現在我喜歡聽中國音樂，買很多中國唱片。

9. 我昨天下課就回家，沒有去圖書館 。

10. 在新年招待會上我認識一位中國留學生。他給我他的地址和電話號。我們喝喝酒，嘗嘗中國菜，談得很高興。

11. 上個月我用中文給爸爸寫一封信 。他很高興，送我一雙冰鞋 。

12. 1994年我在工廠工作。現在我不工作，在加州大學學習。

13. 昨天我沒有上課 ，我去看籃球賽 。加州隊跟德州(Dézhōu, Texas) 隊賽，加州隊又贏 。

READING EXERCISE

沒看書裡的字

小謝: 我要還書。這三本法文書是昨天借 (jiè, to borrow) 的。 那五本德文書是前天借的，這兩本日文書是今天上午借的 。

圖書館員: 你看書看得真快！你會的外語也很多！你一定是個非常好的學生！

小謝: 哪裏。我沒看書裏的字，只 (zhǐ, only) 看了書上的畫兒 。我正在研究外國畫兒呢。還了這些書以後，我還要再借一些有畫兒的外文書 。

LESSON 29

GRAMMAR NOTES

l. The Impending Aspect

The following sentence patterns indicate that an action is going to take place in the imminent future:

1) affirmative	要 / 快 / 快要 / 就要 } V(O) 了	花兒快要開了。 現在三比一，美國隊快贏了！
2) interrogative	affirmative + 嗎?	A: 飛機快要起飛了嗎?
3) negative	沒有。	B: 沒有，九點才起飛 。

To indicate that an action is going to take place very soon, put any of the four adverbs 要, 快, 快要 and 就要 before the predicative verb/adjective and the particle 了 at the end of the sentence, but when there is a time word/phrase before the predicative verb/adjective, only 要 and 就要 can be used:

- 他們明天就要去中國了。
- 比賽十點要開始了。

xx 比賽十點快（要）開始了。 xx

2. The Imperative Sentence

1) To ask somebody to do something:

Verb (Object)!

- 開始!
- 起床!
- 走!
- 給我寫信!

2) To ask somebody not to do something:

别 /不要 Verb (Object)

- 別走，再等一等 。
- 請不要吸煙。

To ask somebody to stop doing something:

别 /不要 Verb (Object) 了

大夫： 以後不要再喝酒了！

老師 ： 別說話了！現在開始上課。

To express a suggestion, advice, request or to make a command sound more polite, add 吧 at the end of the imperative sentences, or add 請 at the beginning of the sentences. Sometimes both are added:

- 請開始！
- 別喝酒了吧 ！
- 請再等一等吧 ！

3. Conjunctions " 因為 (yīnwèi)..., 所以 (suǒyǐ)..."

This is another pair of conjunctions that combines two clauses. The 因為(because) clause gives the cause, and the 所以 (therefore, so) clause shows the effect. Sometimes one of the conjunctions can be omitted.

When the two clauses share one subject, this subject can be placed before or after 因為, or after 所以.

(S1) 因為 (S1)...... , 所以 (S1) ......

- 因為他很努力，所以進步得很快。
- 因為很努力，所以他進步得很快。

When the two clauses have different subjects, the subjects should be positioned after 因為 and 所以 .

因為 (S1)...... , 所以 (S2)......

- 因為 我忘了你的地址, 所以沒有寫信 。
- 因為她的女兒要離開了, 所以她很難過 。

4. The Topic-Comment Sentence

When a subject-predicate construction is used as the predicate of a sentence, this sentence is called a topic-comment sentence. In these kinds of sentences, the subjects serve as the topics, while the predicates comment on the topics. A topic is often followed by more than one comment.

TOPIC	COMMENT
Subject	Predicate (Subject-Predicate construction)

A: 你媽媽 (topic) 身體好嗎? (comment)

B: 她 (topic) 身體很好。 (comment)

A: 你喜歡洛杉磯嗎 ?

B: 洛杉磯 (topic) 車太多, (comment 1) 空氣不好。 (comment 2)

A: 他 (topic) 學習不錯, (comment 1) 工作怎麼樣 ? (comment 2)

B: 他 (topic) 工作也很好。 (comment)

LEARN CHARACTERS

飛(飞) fēi、機(机) jī、場(场) chǎng、身 shēn、體(体) tǐ、

夏 xià、秋 qiū、路 lù、別 bié、離(离) lí、所 suǒ、步 bù、

努 nǔ、力 lì、站 zhàn、注 zhù、放 fàng、忘 wàng、過(过) guò、

* 因 yīn

READING EXERCISE

中文難還是英文難 ？

王老師問一個學中文的美國學生 ： “中文難還是英文難？”

那個學生回答: “中文難！”

王老師又問一個學英文的中國學生 ： “中文難還是英文難？”

那個學生回答: “英文難！”

王老師說： “我想中文和英文都不太難 。很多美國人學中文學得非常好, 很多中國人學英文也學得非常好. 認真、努力 (nǔlì, hard-working) 的學生總是學得很好, 不認真、不努力的學生總是學得不好。”

LESSON 31

GRAMMAR NOTES

l. The Time-Measure Complement

1) The point of time vs. the duration of time

The point of time is expressed by time words which are positioned **before** the main verb.

point of time + V

A: 他每天幾點開始工作？
B: 他每天八點開始工作。

A: 你希望明年幾月去中國？
B: 我希望明年三月去中國。

The duration of time is expressed by a time-measure complement positioned **after** the main verb.

V + duration of time

A: 他每天工作幾個小時 ？
B: 他每天工作八個小時 。

A: 明年你想在中國住幾個月 ？
B: 明年我想在中國住三個月， 去年只住了三天。

2) Sentence patterns using time-measure complement to show the duration of an action are as follows:

A. Without object

S V TM

A: 你想學習多長時間？
B: 我想學習三年。

A: 你在中國工作了多久？

B:　我在中國工作了四年。

The general question words for the duration of time are 多長時間 (duōcháng shíjiān) and 多久 (duōjiǔ).

B. With object

1) S V O V TM

A:　你學中文學了幾年？
B:　我學中文學了三年。

2) S O V TM
3) O S V TM

A:　你中文學了三年，日文也學了三年嗎？
B:　日文我只學了半年。

4) S V TM 的 O

A:　你想學多長時間的日文呢？
B:　我想學兩年的日文。

Pattern 4 is used only when the object is not a personal pronoun and is short and simple. Thus the following sentences are wrong:

xx 他看了三個小時的你昨天買的那本新書。 xx
xx 我等了二十分鐘的他。 xx

C. To negate the above sentences, use 沒(有) for actions that take place in the past, and 不 for actions that take place at present or in the future.

- 日文我不想學三年。
- 我沒有學三年的日文，只學了半年。

D. The modal particle 了 at the end of a sentence with time-measure complement indicates the action is still continuing. Compare the following two sentences:

- 他打了一個小時的電話。
  (He talked on the phone for an hour.)
- 他打了一個小時的電話了。
  (He has been talking on the phone for an hour, and is still talking.)

2. Numerals 幾 and 多 Indicating Approximate Numbers

1) 幾 stands for an indefinite number less than ten, it can stand by itself, be placed after the numeral 十 or before numerals 十, 百 (bǎi, hundred), 千 (qiān, thousand), 萬 (wàn, ten thousand), etc.

	幾	條魚	(several)
十	幾	位華僑	(11-19)
三十	幾	輛車	(31-39)
八十	幾	個學校	(81-89)
	幾	十年	(several dozen / tens of)
	幾	百個語言	(several hundreds)
	幾	千個工廠	(several thousands)
	幾	萬個工人	(several ten-thousands)

2) 多 may be used after the numbers 十, 百, 千, 萬, etc. to indicate an indefinite number and means "more than".

五十	多	把椅子	(more than 50)
一百	多	個國家	(more than 100)
兩千	多	個學生	(more than 2,000)
三萬	多	本書	(more than 30,000)

When the numeral is less than 10, 多 should be placed **between** the measure word and the noun, or **after** a noun which doesn't need a measure word.

兩個	多	小時	xx 兩多個小時 xx
三張	多	紙	xx 三多張紙 xx
四個	多	月	xx 四多個月 xx

五年多, 兩天多

3. Questions with the Adverb 多

The adverb 多 often goes before monosyllabic adjectives such as 大, 長, 遠, 快, to make questions about degree or extent.

- 你今年多大 ?
- 你工作了多長時間了 ?
- 你開車開得多快?

LEARN CHARACTERS

華(华)、僑(侨)、鐘(钟)、首、久、
huá qiáo zhōng shǒu jiǔ

際(际)、言、校、長(长)、希、望、
jì yán xiào cháng xī wàng

第、已、經(经)、
dì yǐ jīng

* 笑、哭、東(东)、西
xiào kū dōng xī

READING EXERCISES

等了二十多分鐘

小謝今天晚上請他女朋友王英看電影 。電影八點開始，小謝七點四十就到電影院了。外邊正在下雨 (xiàyǔ, rain)，小謝不想在外邊等。電影院旁邊有一個酒館 。小謝想：我在酒館等她吧 。小謝進了酒館就想喝酒 。他喝了三瓶啤酒以後，看了看錶 — 啊！八點十分了 ！王英正在電影院前邊等他呢。小謝說："對不起，對不起，我晚了!"王英很不高興，她說："我等你等了二十多分鐘了，真氣人！"小謝說："我八點差二十就來了 。因為你還沒來，所以我去旁邊的酒館 坐了半個小時。"

王英說：“你一定又喝酒了吧 ？”

小謝說: “我只喝了一點兒 ......”

王英說：“昨天我告訴你以後別再喝酒 。今天你就忘了！我不想跟你一起看電影 ， 我要回家 。”

小謝問: “我開車送你回家, 好嗎？”

王英說：“我不要你送。喝了酒的人不可以開車。再見 ！”

河邊餐廳

服務員　幾位？

小張　兩位。

服務員　請在這兒坐。你們要甚麼？

小謝　這是我們第一次來 。請介紹一下你們的菜 。

服務員　我們河邊餐廳的法國魚湯很有名。

小張　好, 我要魚湯。

小謝　我也要魚湯吧 。你們作菜作得快不快？

服務員　不慢， 請等一下兒 。這兒有今天的報, 還有法國雜誌和畫報， 請看吧。我現在就去給你們釣魚 , 沒有魚不能作魚湯 。

小謝　甚麼? 先釣了魚才能作魚湯 ？你要我們等多長時間?

服務員　不用等很長時間, 只要等一個多小時 。

LESSON 32

GRAMMAR NOTES

1. The Aspect of Past Experience with Particle 過

The particle 過 is suffixed to a verb to stress that a certain experience or occurrence did take place in the past. The sentence patterns for the aspect of past experience are as follows:

1) interrogative: V 過 (O) 嗎/沒有?	你住過醫院沒有?
2) affirmative: V 過 (O)	以前住過醫院。
3) negative: 沒(有) V 過 (O) 還沒(有) V 過 (O) 呢	最近沒有住過。 我身體很好，還沒住過醫院呢。

In a sentence with two verbal constructions in a series, 過 is usually placed after the second verb:

V1 (O1) V2 過 (O2)

- 你最近去醫院檢查過身體沒有？
- 去年我去醫院檢查過一次眼睛。
- 我沒開車來過這個地方，今天是第一次 。
- 我還沒用中文寫過作文呢 。

Non-action verbs such as 知道，在，是 can not be suffixed by 過:

xx 我在過那兒兩次。 xx (should be: 我去過那兒兩次。)

xx 我是過足球隊員 。 xx (should be: 我當過足球隊員。)

2. The Time-Measure Complement After Verbs 來/去/到/離開/分別

When a time-measure complement is used after these verbs (and their objects, if any), it indicates the period of time from the occurrence of the actions until the time of speaking; it does not mean that the particular actions lasted for the period of time. For example:

- 我離開日本三年了。 (It's three years since I left Japan.)

- 上了十五分鐘的課了 ，那個學生還沒來。(It's fifteen minutes since the class started, but that student hasn't come yet.)
- 我來加州半年了。(It's half a year since I came to California.)

LEARN CHARACTERS

最、	近、	過(过)、	屋、	眼、	睛、
zuì	jìn	guo	wū	yǎn	jīng

歷(历)、	史、	頭(头)、	醫(医)、	黑
lì	shǐ	tóu	yī	hēi

病、	檢(检)、	查、
bìng	jiǎn	chá

NEW WORDS

(The reading text on P44, PCR is used as the text for this lesson.)

1.	作文	zuòwén	n.	composition
2.	過	guo	par	aspect particle showing past experience
3.	歷史	lìshǐ	n	history
4.	醫學	yīxue	n	medical science
5.	同屋	tóngwū	n	roommate
6.	個子	gèzi	n	size (stature)
7.	頭髮	tóufa	n	hair (on human head)
8.	眼睛	yǎnjing	n	eye
9.	黑	hēi	adj	black
10.	最近	zuìjìn	adv	recently, lately
11.	地方	dìfang	n	place

12.	病	bìng	v,n	be sick, illness
13.	檢查	jiǎnchá	v,n	to check up
	檢查身體			to have a physical examination
14.	醫院	yīyuàn	n	hospital
15.	先	xiān	adv	first

READING EXERCISE

大夫開的藥

古波下了課就回宿舍了。他的同屋小張正在床上休息呢。 小張已經病了兩天了, 古波很不放心。

古波問: “你去過醫院了嗎？”

小張說: “沒有。”

古波說: “你應該請大夫給你檢查一下兒 , 開一點兒藥。”

小張說: “不用去醫院。你看, 桌子上有藥。”

古波看了看桌子上 的藥, 問 : “這是甚麼藥？”

小張說: “上午我哥哥來過了 。這是他給我的藥 。”

古波說: “這不是大夫開 (to prescribe) 的藥 , 你不應該吃。”

小張說: “我哥哥是大夫, 你不知道嗎 ? 他以前是北京醫學院的學生, 現在在紅十字 (Red Cross) 醫院工作。他已經當了兩年的大夫了。”

LESSON 33

GRAMMAR NOTES

1. New Situations or Changed Circumstances Expressed by Modal Particle 了

Examine the difference between the following two dialogs, the modal particle 了 at the end of the sentences in the second dialog indicates a new situation:

A: 你是中學生還是大學生？
B: 我是大學生。(I am a college student.)

A: 你是中學生嗎 ？你今年多大了?
B: 我是大學生了(I am a college student now - I wasn't in the past.)， 我今年十八歲了 。

More examples:

with verbal predicate - 春天到了，不下雪了 。
with adjectival predicate - 樹綠了，天氣暖和了 。
with nominal predicate - 今年 1997 年了，我 20 歲了。

2. Subjectless Sentences

There are more subjectless sentences in Chinese than in English. The most common ones are:

1) about natural phenomena
- 下雨了 。
- 刮風呢。
- 十點了。

2) imperative sentences
- 別走！等一等 ！

3) sentences beginning with verb 有
- 有人認識這個字嗎？(Is there anybody who knows this character?)
- 有人在這兒住嗎？
- 有學生在那兒上課嗎 ？

A: 有人給我打過電話嗎？

B: 沒有(人給你打過電話)。

3. The "從 ... 到 ..."(from ... to ...) Structure

In this structure prepositions 從 and 到 can be followed by time words or place / location words.

從	time /place	到	time /place

- 從你家到我這兒近不近?/遠不遠？
- 從幾月到幾月是秋天 ？
- 我從1996 年到 2000 年在大學學習 。
- 今天上午從九點到十二點我都有課 。
- 我要買一張從洛杉磯到北京的飛機票。
- 從星期一到星期四的報我都有。

LEARN CHARACTERS

雨、雪、刮、風(风)、感、冒、
yǔ xuě guā fēng gǎn mào

樹(树)、葉(叶)、冷 、熱(热)、
shù yè lěng rè

暖、凉、晴、陰(阴)、
nuǎn liáng qíng yīn

* 遠(远)、近、春
yuǎn jìn chūn

NEW WORDS

(The reading text on P69, PCR is used as the text for this lesson.)

1.	天氣	n.	tiānqi	weather
2.	季節	n.	jìjié	season
3.	冷	adj	lěng	cold

4.	刮	v	guā	(the wind) to blow
5.	風	n.	fēng	wind
6.	有時候	adv.	yǒushíhou	sometimes
7.	下	v	xià	(rain, snow, etc.) to fall
8.	雪	n	xuě	snow
9.	最	adv.	zuì	indicates the superlative degree: most/least, highest/lowest
10.	零	num.	líng	zero
11.	度	m.	dù	degree
12.	習慣	n. & v.	xíguàn	habit; to be used to
13.	得	v.	dé	to get, obtain
14.	感冒	n. & v.	gǎnmào	a cold, to catch a cold
15.	暖和	adj.	nuǎnhuo	(of temperature/weather) pleasantly warm
16.	公園	n.	gōngyuán	park
17.	雨	n.	yǔ	rain
18.	熱	adj.	rè	hot
19.	晴	adj.	qíng	(of weather) fine, clear
20.	涼快	adj.	liángkuai	(of temperature/weather) pleasantly cool
21.	樹	n.	shù	tree
22.	葉	n.	yè	leaf
23.	陰	adj.	yīn	(of weather) cloudy
24.	預報	n.	yùbào	forecast
25.	覺得	v.	juéde	to have a feeling that..., to think that...
26.	春天	n.	chūntiān	spring

27.	遠	adj.	yuǎn	far
28.	近	adj	jìn	close

READING EXERCISE

台北(Táiběi)的天氣

很多外國人喜歡春天去台北， 他們説春天是台北最美的季節 。 三、四月的時候花兒開了, 去陽明山 (Yángmíngshān, name of a mountain) 看花兒的人非常多。 夏天很長, 天氣熱極了。每年夏天都刮颱風 (táifēng, typhoon), 刮颱風的時候總是下大雨。台北的秋天不長, 天氣不冷也不熱。冬天不冷， 常常下雨, 可是下得不大 。人們叫這種 (zhǒng, measure word, kind, sort) 雨 “毛毛雨” 。 冬天沒有下過雪 ，最冷的時候也不到零度 。

LESSON 34

GRAMMAR NOTES

l. The Continuous Aspect with Particle 着

l) The particle 着 (zhe) is suffixed to a verb to indicate the continuation of an action or the continuation of the state that is the result of an action. The sentence patterns are as follows:

1)	Place word + V 着 + NP

- 教室的牆上掛 着地圖 。

2)	NP (+ 在 Place word) + V 着

- 地圖在教室的牆上掛 着。

"嗎？" and "沒有？" are used for questions, negative adverbs "沒(有)" and "不"(for habitual actions) are used for negative sentences.

A: 老師坐着嗎?
B: 老師沒有坐着，他在前邊站着。
上課的時候老師不坐 着，他總是站着。

A: 桌子上放着甚麼？
B: 桌子上放着一台 (tái, measure word) 電腦 (diànnǎo, computer)。
A: 也放着電視機嗎？
B: 沒有。

A: 書架 (shūjià, bookshelf)上放 着一封信 ，信封上寫着名字，可是沒有寫 着地址 。
B: 那是昨天我給我朋友寫的信 ，可是不能寄，我忘了他的地址了。

2) In a sentence with verb constructions in a series, the first verb phrase "V1 着 (O1)" indicates the manner or way in which the second verb phrase "V2 (O2)" is performed. In other words, the second verb phrase

indicates the main action, and the first verb phrase describes the accompanying action.

3) V1 着 (O1) V2 (O2)

- 公路上 (on the freeway)有很多人打着電話開車。
- 我弟弟喜歡看着電視吃飯，他也常唱着歌洗澡。(V1 O1 V2 O2)
- 老師在教室前邊站着, 他指着牆上的地圖説：
  "這是長城。"
- 古波拿(ná, take, hold in hand) 着花兒説: "這是送你的。"
  帕蘭卡笑着説: "謝謝! "

3) Since the continuation of an action generally implies that the action is in progress, the above patterns are often combined with patterns indicating an action in progress (正在/正/在...... 呢, or...... 呢).

- 老師正站着上課呢。
- 他們正在那兒等着呢。

4) When 着 is suffixed to a verb to emphasize the continuous aspect, the verb does not take complements after it.

xx 他看着電視看了一個小時。 xx

xx 他開着車開得很快。 xx

5) The "V 着..." phrase can modify a noun/noun phrase:

- 在他前邊坐着看報的那個人你認識嗎？
- 郵局前邊停着的那輛車是誰的？
- 桌子上放着的那些明信片是我在中國買的。
- 正在喝着酒開車的那個人是誰？

2. "Multisyllabic Adjective + Structural Particle 地 (de)" as an Adverbial Modifier.

1) This adverbial modifier should always be placed before the verb. Sometimes the particle 地 is omitted.

- 他努力 (地) 學習。

- 這本書你應該認真(地)看一遍　。

- 老師大聲地問: “ 懂不懂?”

2) Complement of degree describes a present action, an action that has already taken place or happens frequently; it cannot be used to describe an action that has not yet happened. Adverbial modifiers, however, can describe an action that has not occurred.

- 他學得很努力 。(= 他努力地學習 。)

- 我以後也要努力地學習 。

  xx 我以後也要學習得很努力 。xx

3) “Adj + 地 ” expresses the subjective intention while the complement of degree does not.

- 他很高興地來學中文, 可是老師教得不好, 他學得很不高興。

LEARN CHARACTERS

着、封、寄、郵 (邮)、局、收、指、
zhe fēng jì yóu jú shōu zhǐ

牆(墙)、窗、掛(挂)、市、聲(声)、
qiáng chuāng guà shì shēng

* 拿、放、
ná fàng

EXERCISES: Describe the following pictures.

1.

2.

書架
(shūjià)
電腦
(diànnǎo)
燈
(dēng, lamp)
學生宿舍

3.

中國地圖
法國歷史
畫兒
大衣
照片
(zhàopiàn)
信
信封
(xìnfēng)
牀
(chuáng)
古波
中國詩
照像機
(zhàoxiàngjī)
收音機
(shōuyīnjī)
躺
(tǎng, to lie)
紅茶

LESSON 35

GRAMMAR NOTES

l. Summary of the 5 Aspects of an Action

Aspects	Functions (indicating)	Time	Examples
Progressive	an action that is in progress	past present future	- 我進去的時候學生正在考試呢 。 - 現在學生正在考試呢, 沒(有)上課 。 - 明天這時候學生一定正在考試呢 。
Continuous	continuation of an action, or the result of an action	past present future	- 以前桌子上放 着一台電視機 。 - 現在桌子上放着一台電腦，沒（有）放着電視機 。 - 以後桌子上會放着甚麼呢？
Perfect	realization or completion of an action	past present future	- 這本書我們已經學完了。 - 她笑了, 沒(有)不高興。 - 我想放了暑假就回家 。
Impending	an action that is going to take place soon	future	- 我們下星期就要考試了 。 - 快要放暑假了。
Past experience	an action as a past experience	past	- 我只去過中國, 沒(有)去過日本。

2. Review of the Adverbial Modifiers

1) Adverbs:

總是, 已經, 比較, 十分, 非常,一定 , 一起 , 互相,
沒, 不, 別, 常, 很, 也, 都, 先, 太, 真,
才, 就, 又, 還, 再, 更, 最, 多, 只

2) Adjective followed by particle 地:

1.	Disyllabic Adj + 地

認真地，　高興地，　着急地，　大聲地,
放心地，　努力地，　注意地

2.　Adv + Monosyllabic Adj + 地

很好地，更多地，很快地

那個學生很努力地學中文，他上課的時候注意地聽，下課以後認真地複習。老師高興地說：“你是我們班最好的學生! ”

3) Prepositional phrase

給…，從…,　在…,　為…,　跟…,　從… 到…,

- 我媽媽上個月從北京給我寄的書還沒有到。
- 我每天從早上八點到十二點在學校上課。
- 為你的健康乾杯！
- 我常跟中國留學生一起練習口語。

4) Time words

- 哪年？　哪天？	今天, 明天, 那天; 去年, 今年, 明年,
- 哪個月？幾月？	上個月，這個月,下個月，三月,
- 星期幾？	星期一，星期天 (日)
哪個星期？	上 (個)星期, 這(個)星期, 下 (個)星期,
- 甚麼時候？	早上，中午, 下午，晚上， 以前, 現在, 以後，最近,
- 幾點？	三點半

A:　你們大學甚麼時候放暑假?

B:　六月才開始放暑假，你們呢？

A:　我們五月就放。

3. Structural particles 的/得/地

1) 的 is used in attributive modifiers: 的 + N

- 漂亮的郵票
- 爸爸送他的生日禮物

2) 得 is used in complements of degree: V + 得

- 説得很流利
- 考試考得好的學生

3) 地 is used in adverbial modifiers: 地 + V

- 認真地工作
- 着急地等着
- 大聲地説話

4. Review of the Particle 了

1. The **Aspect** Particle 了 is always suffixed to a verb, and is used in the following situations:

l) To **emphasize** the completion of the action .

- 大學隊又贏了！
- 我忘了。

Rules:

a. The object (if any) must be modified. If the object is not modified, the verb must be preceded by an adverbial modifier.

- 我唱了你教我的那個歌。
- 我跟他們一起唱了歌 。

- 他喝了幾杯茶。
- 他在飛機上喝了茶 。

Otherwise the sentence sounds like the first part of a sentence showing sequential actions:

- 我唱了歌(就 ......)
- 他喝了茶(就 ......)

b. Do not use the completion aspect particle 了 when the emphasis of completion is not intended, even though you are talking about actions that already took place in the past:

- 以前我每天喝紅茶 。(past habit)
- 我昨天唱歌的時候沒有人聽 。(V-phrase as modifier)

- 他以前打籃球打得不錯。(complement of degree)

c. In a sentence with verbal constructions in a series, 了 is usually suffixed to the last verb:

- 我昨天開車去中國城買了一本中文詞典 。
  V1 V2 V3

2) Suffixed to the first verb to show sequential actions: after the completion of action l, action 2 took place or will take place. The sentence patterns are as follows:

Future	Vl 了(O1) (就) V2 (O2)
Past	Vl 了(O1) (就) V2 (O2) 了

- 下星期我考了試就回家 。
  V1 V2

- 昨天我下了課去銀行了 。
  V1 V2

2. The **Modal Particle** 了 is used in the following situations:

l) At the end of a sentence to modify the whole sentence, indicating that the event referred to took place in the past and is relevant in the present:

- 你下午去哪兒了？
- 我去看電影了。

Since the action of a past event is often completed, both aspect particle 了 and modal particle 了can appear in the same sentence.

- 我複習了第33課了, 還沒複習第34課呢 。

When the object is modified by a quantitative word or a time measure complement, the sentence implies that the action is on-going.

- 我學了半年的中文了。(I'm still studying.)
- 我們學了35課了。 (We will study more.)

2) At the end of an imperative sentence, asking somebody to stop doing something

- 別再喝酒了！
- 不要說話了!

3) In a sentence showing imminent future

- 我們快要考試了。
- 你們大學快放春假了嗎？

4) At the end of a sentence showing a new situation or changed circumstance

- 不下雨了，天晴了, 我們可以去公園了。
- 我今年十八歲了，是大學生了。

5) In the construction " 太 adj 了 " to show the superlative degree

- 太有意思了！
- 今天的天氣太好了！

LEARN CHARACTERS

考、暑、寒、假、錢(钱)、急、
kǎo shǔ hán jià qián jí

*錶(表)
biǎo

EXERCISES

1. Fill in the blanks with structural particles 的、得、地

1) 帕蘭卡在首都機場 _____ 大廳裏站着。她正着急 _____ 等着她男朋友古波。他們要坐十點 _____ 飛機去上海 。

古波昨天晚上整理行李整理 _____ 太晚了, 所以今天起床起 _____ 很晚。帕蘭卡從機場給他打電話 _____ 時候, 他正看着今天 _____ 報吃早飯呢 。帕蘭卡不高興 _____ 說: "你總是起 _____ 太晚, 真氣人! 別吃早飯了，我們 _____ 飛機快要起飛了。" 古波說: "你放心, 我吃 _____ 很快。十分鐘以後我就出發 。 我同屋要開他 _____ 新車送我，他開_____ 很快。 現在八點半, 我九點半一定能到機場 。" 帕蘭卡大聲_____ 說: "你 _____ 錶不對, 現在已經

九點半了。”

2) 葉子是我們學校 _____ 日本留學生, 她每次考試都考 _____ 很好, 是個很努力 _____ 學生。今天是春假 _____ 第一天，上午我跟她去學校旁邊 _____ 體育館游泳。

在體育館, 葉子高興_____ 指着她 _____ 新游泳衣説：“你看，這是我昨天買 _____ ，你覺得怎麼樣？” 我説: “很漂亮！我 _____ 太舊了, 我也想買一件新 _____ 。” 她讓我去她常去 _____ 那家日本商店買。她説那兒 _____ 營業員總是很熱情_____ 幫助買東西 _____ 人。

葉子雖然游 _____ 很快, 可是我覺得她游 _____ 不好看。我游 _____不太快, 可是游 _____ 比較好看。我們正在休息 _____ 時候, 有人大聲 _____ 叫我們 。那是我們兩個人都認識 _____ 中國同學王華， 他是我們系游泳游 _____ 最好 _____人，所以我們請他教我們怎樣游泳。他熱情 _____ 回答: “好, 我們開始吧。”

2. Fill in the blanks with appropriate particles, adverbs or sentence conjunctions **when necessary**.

1. 古波學_____ 五個月 _____ 日文 _____ 。帕蘭卡沒有學 _____ 日文 ____ 。
2. 那兩個日本學生念中國詩念 _____ 真好聽。他們學中文已經學_____ 兩年 _____ 。我以前沒有聽 _____ 日本人念中國詩_____。
3. 現在是暑假 _____ 。不用去上學 _____ 。天氣真好, 我們可以開車去墨西哥 (Mòxīgē, Mexico) 玩兒。我還沒有去 _____ 墨西哥呢。
4. A: 最近你檢查 _____ 身體嗎?

4. A: 最近你檢查 _____ 身體嗎?

   B: 沒有。最近我去 ____ 一次中國 。上星期 ____ 回來。

5. 到 _____ 中國以後，帕蘭卡很想家，因為她沒離開 _____ 媽媽 。 古波常常跟她說： “ 別難過 _____ ， 給媽媽打一個電話 _____ 。

6. 我 _____ 窗子前邊有一張桌子，兩把椅子. 桌子上邊有我已經看 _____ 的一本書和我還沒有用 _____ 的一本新詞典 。

7. 春天到 _____ , 花都開 _____ ， 外邊也不冷 _____ ， 我們可以去海邊玩兒 _____。

8. A: 你游泳游 _____ 怎麼樣?

   B: _____ 我非常喜歡游泳， _____ 我游 _____ 不好。古波游 _____ 很好。古波的女朋友帕蘭卡游 _____ 更好。

9. 前天我下 _____ 課 _____ 去看足球賽 _____ 。小張來 ____ 找 _____ 我三次，我都不在 。我的同屋也都去 _____ 看電影 _____ 。昨天我下 _____課就 _____ 去跳舞 _____ 。我跳 _____ 一個晚上 。我的同屋也去踢 _____ 一個晚上的足球 。小張又來找我 _____ 。_____ 我又不在 ____ ， ____ 他很不高興。

READING EXERCISE

借 書

小謝 你昨天買的那本小說真有意思 ， 我可以借 (jiè, borrow) 嗎 ?

小張 你又要借我的書 ? 從去年到現在你已經從我這兒借了很多書了。

小謝 不太多啊, 我只借了二十多本 。我知道你學中文 ,

小張　　你應該去圖書館借書，或者去書店買書。我不是你的圖書館。你甚麼時候還我那些書？

小謝　　別着急，你有空兒看的時候我一定還　。我女朋友王英很喜歡看小説，那些書都在她那兒呢。她是醫學院的學生，也很忙，書她還沒開始看呢，我想放了暑假她就會開始看。

PART II

HOMEWORK

HOMEWORK (Lesson 21)

Name ____________

Section ____________

T. A. ____________

I. Translate the following sentences into Chinese.

1. Who is the teacher that teaches you Chinese grammar?

2. The novels that I like to read are all written by English writers (zuòjiā).

3. The bunch of flowers that you gave me is really pretty.

4. Do you know that pretty girl who is dancing with Gubo?

5. The birthday present my dad gave me last year was a new car.

II. Translate the following dialogs into Chinese.

1. A: Is it your birthday today?
   B: No, my birthday is May the 2nd. It is my younger sister's birthday today. Look, these are the birthday gifts her friends gave her.

2. A: How old is your younger brother?
   B: He is 14 this year.
   A: How old is your father?
   B: He is 52 this year.

3. A: The Japanese car he bought yesterday is new, - a 1996 model.
B: Mine is even newer. Mine is a 1997 model.

III. Fill in the blanks with 吧 ，嗎, 呢

1. A: 明天晚上你有事兒 ____?

B: 沒事兒，你____?

A: 我也沒事兒，跟我一起去跳舞 ____。

2. 女兒： 媽媽，我二十歲生日的時候，你送我一輛車，好____?

媽媽： 好____。你要日本的還是美國的？

女兒： 給我買一輛紅的日本車 ____。

IV. Fill in the blanks with the following verbs. Reduplicate the verbs to soften the tones, and to indicate relaxed and informal actions.

問, 聽, 看, 介紹, 休息, 穿

1. 姐姐，讓我 ______ 你的新裙子，好嗎?

2. 晚飯以後，我想 ______ 音樂，______ 電視(diànshì, TV).

3 王老師，請您給我們 ________ ________ 北京大學。

4. 明天我不想去看電影，我想在家 ________ ________ 。

5. 這個字我也不認識，你 ______ 王老師吧。

HOMEWORK (Lesson 22)

Name ________________

Section ________________

T. A. ________________

I. Translate the following phrases into Chinese:

1. the garden behind the house/ the house behind the garden

2. inside the bedroom/ outside the kitchen

3. the room in the middle/ in the middle of the room

4. the window in the front/ in front of the window

5. on the desk/ under the desk

II. Translate the following dialogs into Chinese.

1. A: Excuse me. Where is the library?
   B: I am going to the library too. Please follow (come with) me. Look! The library is there, - next to the bank.

2. A: How many bedrooms are there in your house?
   B: There are three bedrooms behind the living-room. The big one in the middle is my parents'; the one on the right is my younger sister's; and the one on the left is mine.

3. A: Does your mom ask you to help her with cooking?
   B: My mom never allows me to cook in the kitchen. She always says: "Go to the study and do your homework (zuòyè)."

4. A: When will you clean up (tidy up) the garage?
   B: At the time when you clean up the bathroom, I will clean up the garage.

5. A: Where do you usually eat dinner?
   B: Sometimes we eat in the kitchen; sometimes we eat in the dining room next to the kitchen.

III. Reading exercise: Read the following passage and then translate it into English.

看，這張照片 (zhàopiàn, photo)是我在北京大學留學生宿舍的房間。 我的桌子在窗戶前邊。窗戶外邊有一個漂亮的花園 。吃晚飯以前， 我常常在那個花園裏看書， 聽音樂。

VI. Composition: Write a passage of at least six sentences with position words to describe your room or your house.

V. Translate the following questions into Chinese, and then answer them according to the map given. Please answer in complete sentences.

1. Where is the café?

2. Is the restaurant between the bank and the store?

3. Where is the library?

4. Is there a factory in front of the post office?

5. What is the building facing the library?

6. What is there to the left of the café?

7. Is there a movie theater next to the Foreign Language Institute?

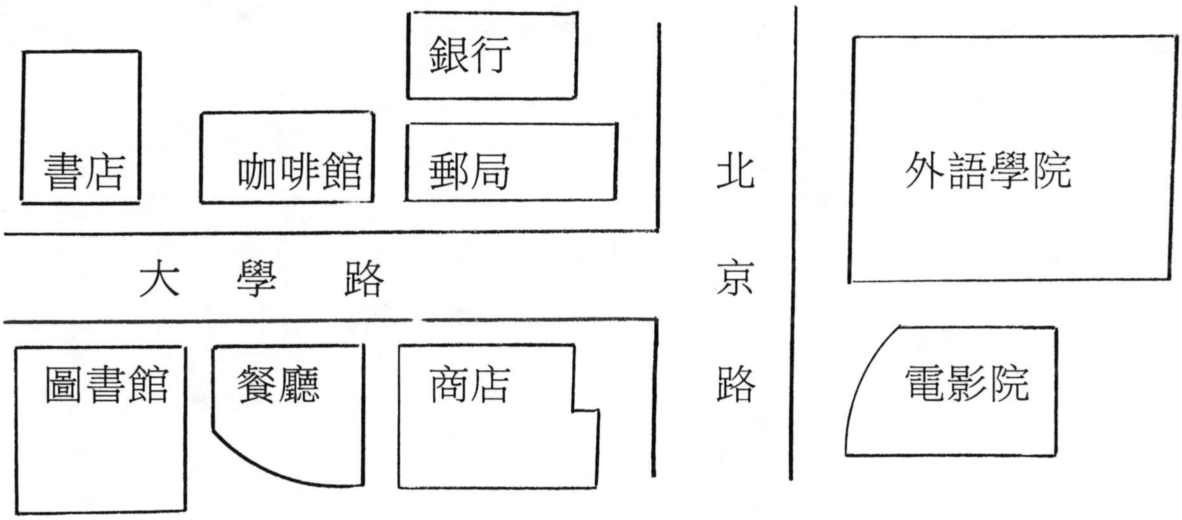

HOMEWORK (Lesson 23)

Name ________________

Section ________________

T. A. ________________

I. Write a phone conversation: Your friend was not home; his roommate answered the phone. You asked him to tell your friend to call you back, and you told him your name and phone number.

II. Translate the following dialogs into Chinese.

1. A: Was Ding Yun watching TV when you called her this afternoon?
   B: No, she was reviewing English grammar .

2. A: What does the TV news say?
   B: The US student delegation is now visiting Beijing University, and they will visit some Chinese professors tomorrow.

3. A: Are you free this evening? Let's go to Chinatown to watch a Chinese movie.
   B: Great! When do we go?
   A: How about 7:00? I will drive over to your place to pick you up. (to pick up - jiē)

IV. Describe the picture below, using sentences of progressive aspect where possible.

HOMEWORK (Lesson 25)

Name ____________________

Section ____________________

T. A. ____________________

I. Translate the following questions into Chinese and then answer them according to the information given.

	古波	帕蘭卡
游泳	快	慢
說中文	不錯	流利
寫漢字	不好	很漂亮
跳舞	不太好	非常好
起床	九點	六點

1. Does Gubo swim slowly?

2. How (well) do Gubo and Palanka speak Chinese?

3. How (well) do they write Chinese characters?

4. How (well) do they dance?

5. Does Palanka get up late?

II. Arrange the following words into gramatically correct sentences.

1. 你/ 認識 / 那個人/ 跟王老師/ 說話 / 正在 / 的/ 嗎?

2. 我/ 買的/ 昨天/ 那些/ 在 / 中文書/ 桌子上。

3. 你朋友 / 得 / 認真 / 不/ 工作 / 認真?

4. 我/ 都/ 語法 / 不懂/ 教的/ 老師 / 上課的時候 / 今天。

III. Translate the following dialogs into Chinese.

1. A: How (well) did you sleep last night?
   B: I did not sleep too well. I got up very late this morning.

2. A: I'd like to have a little more of the fish soup. You cooked the fish soup really well.
   B: It's nothing. My wife cooks (it) even better.

V. Composition: Write an essay (of at least 8 sentences) about a friend of yours. The essay should include sentences of complement of degree.

HOMEWORK (Lesson 26)

Name ________________

Section ________________

T. A. ________________

I. Complete the following dialogs with affirmative-negative (V 不 V) questions. Use optative verbs in the questions.

1. A: ____?

   B: 以後我不想研究中國文學。

2. A: ____?

   B: 學中文的學生應該常常跟中國人一起練習說中文 。

3. A: ____?

   B: 明天晚上你不能借我的車 ， 我自己(zìjǐ, oneself)要用。

4. A: ____?

   B: 今天回家以後，我要休息一下兒 。

5. A: ____?

   B: 我現在還不會看中文雜誌呢。

6. A: ____?

   B: 今天我沒空兒， 明天我願意幫你洗車 。

7. A: ____?

   B: 晚上十點以後 ，你不能給我打電話。 我睡覺睡得早。

II. Translate the following dialogs into Chinese.

1. A: Do you wish to be an interpreter in the future?

   B: No. I want to do research on French literature, but I don't know whether I should study fiction or poetry.

2. A: I plan to go to China to do research on the famous Chinese writer Lu Xun's novels.
B: Can you go this year?
A: Yes, I can go as early as this September. I will come back to this country (回國) in November or December of next year.

3. A: Although I often go to bed as late as 12:30, I always get up as early as 5:00 in the morning (早上 , zǎoshang).
B: You do not get enough sleep. (You sleep too little.)

4. A: Can you read Chinese newspapers?
B: No. I should be able to read Chinese newspapers as early as next year. Next year will be the third year that I study Chinese.

5. A: I am looking for an ideal job, but I know it is not easy.
B: You speak Chinese fluently. You can be a Chinese language teacher or interpreter.

6. A: Is he willing to help me?
B: I think he is willing to, but I don't know whether he has time.

7. A: Do you want to be an interpreter or a writer?
B: I don't want to be an interpreter or a writer. I want to be a doctor or an engineer.

III. Comment on Gubo's schedule and Palanka's schedule. Use 才 and 就 to show earliness or lateness as appropriate.

Activities	Gubo	Palanka
get up	9:00 am	6:00 am
go to school	11:00 am	8:00 am
have supper	6:00 pm	8:00 pm
go to bed	11:50 pm	10:00 pm

1. ________________________________ , ____________________________________

2. ________________________________ , ____________________________________

3. ________________________________ , ____________________________________

4. ________________________________ , ____________________________________

HOMEWORK (Lesson 27)

Name ____________________

Section ____________________

T. A. ____________________

I. Change the following statements into questions and give negative answers.

e.g. 他來了。

他來了沒有？/他來了嗎？

他沒有來。

1. 他們問了老師很多問題。

2. 我在北京認識了一些新朋友。

3. 昨天的舞會上小謝喝了很多中國葡萄酒。

III. Insert 了 into the following sentences **when necessary.**

1. 昨天晚上我喝五瓶啤酒。
2. 你聽今天的新聞沒有？
3. 美國代表團昨天參觀哪個大學？
4. 昨天我沒有整理書房。
5. 丁雲作的那個中國菜你嘗沒有？
6. 我用中文給媽媽寫一封 (fēng, measure word)信，她很高興。
7. 我去年常常開車去中國城看電影。

IV. Translate the following sentences into Chinese.

1. Yesterday we went to the Chinese embassy to attend a reception. I drank a glass of (grape) wine and also tasted some Chinese dishes. I did not use chopsticks because (yīnwèi) I did not know how to (not able to).

2. A: I am really glad that we can come to see this famous movie. Has it started yet?
B: It has not started yet. It won't start until 5:00. Let's go downstairs to have a cup of coffee.

3. A: He is a very famous writer, but he has not written many books.
B: Although he writes slowly, he writes well.

V. Fill in the blanks with 又, 再, or 還.

1. 我很喜歡這件上衣，我想 _____ 買一件 。
2. 昨天我給他打了電話，他不在。 今天我去找他，他 _____ 不在。
3. 這本書非常有意思，我以後 _____ 想 _____ 看一遍 。
4. 丁雲昨天沒有來上中文課 ，今天 _____ 沒有來。
5. 今天來看電影的人太多了， 我不想排隊，我們明天 _____ 來看吧。
6. 這個電影沒有意思，我不想 _____ 看。
7. 你作的魚湯真好喝 ，我_____ 要_____ 喝一點兒 。
8. 去年我去了兩次歐洲 (Ōuzhōu, Europe)， 今年我沒 _____ 去。

HOMEWORK (Lesson 28)

Name ________________

Section ________________

T. A. ________________

I. Insert 了 in the following sentences at the proper positions.

1. 上 個 月 我 回 紐 約 (Niǔyuē, New York)看 我 爸 爸 媽 媽 。
2. 昨 天 你 在 商 店 買 幾 雙 新 鞋 ?
3. 今 天 晚 上 我 看 電 視 新 聞 就 睡 覺 。
4. 去 年 你 去 歐 洲 玩 兒 沒 有 ?

II. Answer the following questions according to the facts.

1. 昨天晚上你去哪兒了?

   ____

2. 上星期六你看電影了沒有 ?

   ____

3. 昨天下了中文課你作甚麼了?

   ____

4. 今天吃了晚飯你去哪兒 ?

   ____

III. Translate the following dialogs into Chinese.

1. A: Your elder brother is not home again. Where did he go?
   B: He went to the Chinese Embassy to attend a party. He called you this afternoon and you were not home either. Where did you go?
   A: Right after I had lunch, I went to watch the basketball game.
   B: Did the Lakers (húrén) team win?
   A: They played extremely well, but they lost - 90 to 98. The referees were not fair. I was very upset.

2. A: Where do you plan to go this weekend (周末, zhōumò)?
B: Tomorrow I am going to ski (滑雪, huá xuě)right after I eat breakfast. Yesterday I went to the store and bought a ski hat.

3. A: What (kind of) sports do you like?
B: I like playing tennis. I also play table tennis often.
A: Do you know how to ice skate? In winter you can skate in Beijing.
B: I knew how to skate (as early as) when I was seven years old. My ice skates are too small now. I should buy a new pair.

IV. Reading exercise: Read the following passage and then translate it into English.

昨天下午加州大學隊跟德州 (Dézhōu, Texas) 大學隊有一場足球賽。古波和帕蘭卡一起去看比賽。 這兩個隊都踢得很好、很認真。

帕蘭卡問古波: "你想哪個隊會贏 ?" 古波回答: "我想加州大學隊一定會贏 !" 帕蘭卡說: "可是我想他們會輸。" 古波說: "你不懂足球 ! "

HOMEWORK (Lesson 29)

Name ________________

Section ________________

T. A. ________________

I. Translate the following phrases into Chinese.

1. every spring/ last summer/ this winter/ next fall

2. to tour Europe by ship/ to travel to Asia by airplane

3. to see my friend off at the airport/ to pick up my friend at the railway station

4. to get off the bus/ to get on the plane

II. Translate the following dialogs into Chinese.

1. A: The plane is going to take off soon.
   B: Don't forget to call me as soon as you arrive in China.
   A: I definitely will. Take care of yourself (lit. pay attention to your body).
   B: Don't worry (lit. be at ease). Have a safe trip!

2. A: How (well) does Ding Yun work?
   B: She works extremely conscientiously and studies very hard; therefore she makes progress very fast. She is also very willing to help her classmates.

3. A: We are going to part (to be separated from each other). I really don't want to leave you.
   B: Don't be sad. We will be able to see each other again as early as this summer or fall.

4. The doctor says: "Don't drink wine any more. Stop smoking. Do not drink too much coffee. Do not stay up too late."

5. Before we got on the plane, my dad wanted to take pictures for us. He asked everybody to stand a little closer and took many pictures.

III. Connect the two clauses into one sentence, using "因為 ...所以..." or "雖然 ...但是 ..."

1. 我爸爸想讓我當大夫。我想當老師。

2. 我忘了你的電話號。沒有給你打電話。

3. 中文系的學生很多。老師很少。

4. 他明天要去機場接他媽媽 。他不能來上課 。

IV Write a passage of about ten sentences about a city/ a school/ a person that you are familiar with. Try to use topic-comment sentences.

e.g. 我爸爸 (topic) 身體很好。(comment)

我們學校 (topic) 食堂的飯太難吃了。(comment)

HOMEWORK (Lesson 31)

Name ________________
Section ________________
T. A. ________________

I. Answer the following questions in complete sentences according to the information given.

1. 你每天幾點去學校？(7:30 a.m.)

2. 你昨天看了多長時間的電視？(1.5 hours)

3. 你每天甚麼時候回家？(2:15 p.m.)

4. 你昨天晚上睡覺睡了多久？(more than 8 hours)

5. 你踢足球踢了多少年了？(more than 4 years)

6. 你每星期工作多長時間？(20 hours)

III. Translate the following sentences into Chinese.

1. A: How long do you plan to stay in Beijing?
   B: I'd like to stay there for several months. This is the third time I came back (returned) to Beijing. The first time I stayed for more than twenty days. The second time I taught English at Beijing Language Institute for more than four weeks. There were several dozen students in my class.

2. An old overseas Chinese arrived at the Capital International Airport in Beijing this morning. His friend did not come to pick him up until he had waited for more than an hour.

3. A: You speak Chinese extremely well.
   B: Oh, far from it.
   A: How long have you been studying Chinese?
   A: I have been studying Chinese for over two years.

IV. Reading exercise: Read the following passage and then translate it into English.

今天古波要請他去年在 北京認識的幾個朋友來他家吃晚飯，他請他媽媽給他們作飯　。古波的媽媽作飯作得很慢　。她吃了早飯就開始準備。她作面包作了三個小時　，作火腿作了兩個多小時 。古波說：“媽媽 ， 您能不能快一點兒？我請的客人很快就要來了 !” 古波的媽媽說：“要是你願意　，你可以來幫幫我!” 古波回答：“媽媽 ， 我只(zhǐ, only) 會吃 ，不會作!”

HOMEWORK (Lesson 32)

Name ________________

Section ________________

T. A. ________________

I. Answer the following questions in complete sentences according to your experience.

1. 你以前去過中國嗎？

2. 你開過飛機沒有？

3. 你最近去醫院檢查過身體嗎？

4. 你在中學的時候學過中文嗎？

5. 你看過很多中國電影嗎？

6. 你今年得過病沒有？

7. 你用中文寫過信嗎？

8. 你喝過中國啤酒嗎？

III. Translate the following sentences into Chinese.

1. A: It has been six months since you came to Europe. Have you been to France?

   B: No, I haven't, but I have been to Britain twice.

2. My doctor recently told me to go to Capital Hospital to have a physical exam, but I don't know where the hospital is. My roommate is a medical school student. He has worked at the Capital Hospital before. He is going to give me the address of the hospital.

3. A: How long have you been studying Chinese?
   B: I have already been studying Chinese for over five months, but I haven't written a composition in Chinese yet. I think I should try.

IV. Write a composition (of about 10 sentences) about something interesting that happened to you in the past. (Use sentences with particle 過.)

HOMEWORK (Lesson 33)

Name ____________________

Section ____________________

T. A. ____________________

I. Translate the following phrases into Chinese.

1. the hottest season of a year

   the rainy season

2. the plane ticket from Japan to America

   the train (huǒchē) from Washington D. C. (Huáshèngdùn) to New York (Niǔyuē)

3. from the first week to the fifth week

   from Monday to Friday

4. six degrees

   six degrees below zero

II. Answer the following questions in complete sentences.

1. 今年是一九九七年嗎 ？

2. 昨天很熱，今天涼快了嗎？

3. 上學期 (last quarter/semester) 你很忙，這學期你不太忙了吧？

4. 昨天有人到你家找過你嗎 ？

5. 從你家到學校近不近？

6. 你班 (bān, class) 上有人姓張嗎 ？

III. Translate the following dialogs into Chinese.

1. A: It is raining. We can't go to the park now.
   B: The weather forecast says it will be clear tomorrow. Let's go tomorrow.

2. Winter has come. The wind is blowing everyday. Sometimes it reaches ten degrees below zero. From December to February it often snows. Some people like to go skiing, but I think (feel) it is too cold outside and it is more interesting to watch TV at home. This is my first winter in Beijing. I should take care of myself (lit. pay attention to my body).

3. A: I attend the Japanese class from 8:00 to 9:00 every morning. I think (feel) that Japanese is very difficult, but I'm already used to it now.
   B: It is already 7:45 now. You should go to class now.

IV. Write a composition (of about 10 sentences) about the weather of your hometown.

HOMEWORK (Lesson 34)

Name ________________

Section ________________

T. A. ________________

I. Fill in the blanks with an appropriate verb and the continuous aspect particle.

1. 古波的桌子上 _______ 兩本漢語詞典。

2. 我的床對面的牆上 _______一張我爸爸媽媽的照片 。

3. 我每天晚上都 _______ 咖啡聽音樂 。

4. 張老師今天_______ 一件新襯衫來上課 。

5. 丁雲的媽媽 _______ 丁雲給她寫的信， 高興地笑了。

6. 丁雲的門 _______， 我想她一定在家 。

II. Translate the following sentences into Chinese.

1. I went to the post office at Tian'anmen Square to mail two letters. A sign is hanging on window no. 3. "Air mail and registered mail" is written on the sign. The clerk, pointing at the poster on the wall, told me how to write a Chinese envelope.

2. There are many students in the library. Some are sitting there reading magazines, some are standing there looking for books. Outside the library, some are talking loudly and some are singing happily.

III. Fill in the envelope given below according to the following information: Li Mei, who lives at 362 Beijing Road, Shanghai, 200031, writes a letter to his friend Wang Jin, who lives at 443 Guoji Road, Nanjing 210093.

— — — — — —

收信人地址 ______________________________

____

收信人姓名 ______________________________ 收

寄信人地址姓名

____

______________________________ 寄

— — — — —

IV. Write a passage of at least 6 sentences to describe picture no.3 on page 50. Use location words and continuous aspect with 着 where applicable.

HOMEWORK (Lesson 35)

Name ________________

Section ________________

T. A. ________________

I. Fill in the blanks with particles 的, 地 , 得, 過, 着, 了; prepositions 從, 到, 給, 在, 跟...一起 ; adverbs 才, 就; or conjunctions 雖然 ...可是..., 因為 ...所以 ....

1. 他開車開 ________ 太快, ________ 我不喜歡坐他 ________車。

2. 我每天晚上 ______ 六點 ___ 八點 ___ 中國餐館工作。

3. 我感冒 ______ 。我以前沒得 _____ 感冒。

4. ______ 我三歲就會游泳， ______ 我三十三歲才學滑冰 。

5. 姐姐 ____ 法國 ____ 我寄來 ______ 那本雜誌非常有意思。

6. 他以前常 ______ 他同學 ______ 去古波那兒 ______ 啤酒聽音樂， ______ 現在他不去 ______。

7. ______他上課 ______ 時候總是很注意 ______ 聽, 下課以後又很認真 ______ 複習, ______ 他學 ____ 非常好。

II. Translate the following dialogs into English.

1. A: During the summer vacation last year, I went to Europe with my roommate. We visited six countries. Where did you go?

   B: I didn't leave Los Angeles. My parents came to visit me from Beijing. They stayed with me at my place for more than three weeks. After they went back to China, I worked in the student bookstore for more than a month.

2. A: We will have our examination next week. I am worried, because I have not reviewed very well. I take five courses (measure word for course - 門, mén) this quarter; I am very busy.
B: Don't worry. We can review together. I am willing to help you.

3. A: Who are these people in this photo?
B: The woman who is holding a bunch of flowers is my elder sister; and the man who is standing behind her is her husband. The boy sitting in the front is their son (兒子; érzi).

4. A: What was Gubo doing when you went to his dorm this afternoon?
B: He was lying in bed reading a novel that he bought yesterday.

APPENDIX A

TEXTS (LESSONS 21-35) IN TRADITIONAL CHARACTERS

第二十一課課文　　這 束 花 兒 真 好 看

(Pàlánkǎ jiā. Dīng Yún jìn.)
(帕蘭卡 家。丁　雲　進。)

Dīng Yún: Zhù nǐ shēngrì hǎo! Zhè shì sòng nǐ de huār.
丁　雲：祝　你 生日　好！這　是 送　你 的 花兒。

Pàlánkǎ: À, zhèshù huār zhēn hǎokàn, fēicháng gǎnxiè. Jīntiān
帕蘭卡：啊，這束　花兒 真　好看，　非常　　感謝。今天

lái de tóngxué hěn duō, wǒ zhēn gāoxìng. qǐng jìn.
來 的 同學　很　多，我 真　　高興。 請 進。

Dīng Yún: Bùlǎng Xiānsheng, Bùlǎng Tàitai, nǐmen hǎo!
丁　雲：布朗　　先生、　布朗　太太，　你們 好！

Bùlǎng: Nǐ hǎo. Qǐng zuò.
布　朗：你 好。 請　坐。

Tàitai: Dīng Yún zhēn niánqīng. Nǐ jīnnián duō dà?
太　太：丁　　雲　真　年輕。　你 今年　多 大？

Dīng Yún: Wǒ jīnnián èrshíèrsuì.
丁　雲：我　今年　二十二歲。

Tàitai: Nǐ de shēngri shì nǎ yìtiān?
太　太：你 的 生日　是　哪　一天？

Dīng Yún: Wǒ de shēngri shì èryuè shíliùrì.
丁　雲：我 的 生 日 是　二月　十六日。

Pàlánkǎ: Dīng Yún, tāmen dōu zài nàr tiào wǔ. Nǐ kàn, nàge
帕蘭卡：丁　　雲，他們　都 在 那兒 跳 舞。你　看，那個

niánqīng de gūniang shì Rìběn rén, wǒ gěi nǐmen
年輕 的 姑娘 是 日本 人， 我 給 你們

jièshaojièshao.
介紹 介紹。

Dīng Yún: Hǎo. Bùlǎng Xiānsheng, nín zuò, Wǒmen qù kànkan tā.
丁 雲： 好。 布朗 先生， 您 坐，我們 去 看看 她。

Bùlǎng: Qǐng ba.
布 朗： 請 吧。

Tàitai: Zhège Zhōngguó gūniang hěn piàoliang.
太 太： 這個 中國 姑娘 很 漂亮。

Bùlǎng: Wǒ shuō Pàlánkǎ gèng piàoliang.
布 朗： 我 說 帕蘭卡 更 漂亮。

Tàitai: Shì ma?
太 太： 是 嗎？

Bùlǎng: Tā xiàng tā māma.
布 朗： 她 像 她 媽媽。

Tàitai: Shéi a? Wǒ qù kāi mén. À, shì Wáng Lǎoshī, qǐng jìn.
太 太： 誰啊？ 我 去 開 門。啊，是 王 老師， 請 進。

第二十二課課文 後 邊 有 一 個 小 花 園

Tàitai: Qǐng Dīng Yún kànkan wǒmen de xīn fángzi ba.
太 太： 請 丁 雲 看看 我們 的 新 房子 吧。

Pàlánkǎ: Hǎo. Dīng Yún, gēn wǒ lái. Zhè shì kètīng.
帕蘭卡： 好。 丁 雲， 跟 我 來。這 是 客廳。

Dīng Yún: Zhège kètīng hěn dà, yě hěn piàoliang.
丁 雲： 這個 客廳 很 大， 也 很 漂亮。

Tàitai: Kètīng pángbiān shì shūfáng. Qǐng jìn.
太 太： 客廳 旁邊 是 書房。 請 進。

Pàlánkǎ: Zhèr yǒu yǐzi, zuò ba.
帕蘭卡： 這兒 有 椅子，坐 吧。

Dīng Yún: Xièxie. Nǐmen de shū zhēn bù shǎo.
丁 雲： 謝謝。 你們 的 書 真 不 少。

Pàlánkǎ: Zhuōzi shàngbiān de shū dōu shì bàba de. Tā zǒng
帕蘭卡： 桌子 上邊 的 書 都 是 爸爸 的。 他 總

bú ràng wǒmen zhěnglǐ.
不 讓 我們 整理。

Tàitai: Qù kànkan wǒmen de chúfáng ba. Chúfáng zài duìmiàn,
太 太： 去 看看 我們 的 廚房 吧。 廚房 在 對面，

cóng zhèr zǒu.
從 這兒 走。

Pàlánkǎ: Dīng Yún, wǒmen de chúfáng tài xiǎo.
帕蘭卡： 丁 雲，我們 的 廚房 太 小。

Tàitai: Bù xiǎo — zuò fàn de zǒngshi wǒ yíge rén.
太 太： 不 小 — 作 飯 的 總是 我 一個 人。

Pàlánkǎ: Hǎo le, māma, yǐhòu wǒ yídìng bāngzhù nǐ zuò fàn.
帕蘭卡： 好 了，媽媽，以後 我 一定 幫助 你 作 飯。

Tàitai: Xièxie nǐ. Cāntīng zài chúfáng zuǒbiān, lǐbiān de
太 太： 謝謝 你。 餐廳 在 廚房 左邊， 裏邊 的

fángjiān shì wǒmen de wòshì.
房間 是 我們 的 臥室。

Pàlánkǎ: Hòubiān hái yǒu yíge xiǎo huāyuán.
帕蘭卡： 後邊 還 有 一個 小 花園。

Dīng Yún: Pàlánkǎ, nǐ de wòshì zài nǎr?
丁 雲： 帕蘭卡, 你 的 臥室 在 哪兒？

Pàlánkǎ: Wǒ de wòshì zài kètīng zuǒbiān. Nà shì xǐzǎojiān.
帕蘭卡： 我 的 臥室 在 客廳 左邊。 那 是 洗澡間。

Wǒmen de xīn fángzi zěnmeyàng?
我們 的 新 房子 怎麼樣？

Dīng Yún: Nǐmen de xīn fángzi fēicháng hǎo.
丁 雲： 你們 的 新 房子 非常 好。

第二十三課課文 我 正 在 看 電 視 呢

Pàlánkǎ: Wèi, shì xuésheng sùshè ma?
帕蘭卡： 喂，是 學生 宿舍 嗎？

Gōngrén: Shì a. Nín zhǎo shéi?
工　人： 是啊。您 找 誰？

Pàlánkǎ: Wǒ zhǎo Dīng Yún, qǐng tā jiē diànhuà.
帕蘭卡： 我 找 丁 雲， 請 她 接 電話。

Gōngrén: Hǎo, qǐng děngyiděng.
工　人： 好， 請 等一等。

Dīng Yún: Wèi, wǒ shì Dīng Yún. Nǐ shì Pàlánkǎ ba?
丁　雲： 喂， 我 是 丁 雲。 你 是 帕蘭卡 吧？

Pàlánkǎ: Duì le, nǐ zài xiūxi ma?
帕蘭卡： 對 了，你 在 休息 嗎？

Dīng Yún: Méiyou, wǒ zài fùxí kèwén ne, nǐ ne?
丁　雲： 沒有， 我 在 複習 課文 呢，你 呢？

Pàlánkǎ: Wǒ zài jiāli. Wǒ zhèngzài kàn diànshì ne.
帕蘭卡： 我 在 家裏。 我 正在 看 電視 呢。

Dīng Yún: Yǒu shénme xīnwén?
丁　雲： 有 甚麼 新聞？

Pàlánkǎ: Zhōngguó yǒuhǎo dàibiǎotuán zhèngzài cānguān yíge
帕蘭卡： 中國 友好 代表團 正在 參觀 一個

gōngchǎng, gōngrénmen zhèng huānyíng tāmen ne.
工廠， 工人們 正 歡迎 他們 呢。

Dīng Yún: Nǐmen de dàibiǎotuán yě zài Zhōngguó fǎngwèn ne,
丁　雲： 你們 的 代表團 也 在 中國 訪問 呢，

bàoshang yǒu tāmen de zhàopiàn. Gǔbō ne? Tā zěnmeyàng?
報上 有 他們 的 照片。 古波呢？他 怎麼樣？

Pàlánkǎ: Tā bú zài, tā zǒngshì hěn máng. Xiàwǔ wǒ gěi tā dǎ
帕蘭卡： 他 不 在，他 總是 很 忙。 下午 我 給 他 打

diànhuà de shíhou, tā zhèng shàng kè ne. Wèi, wǒ shuō,
電話 的 時候，他 正 上 課 呢。 喂，我 說，

míngtiān nǐ yǒu kòngr ma?
明天 你 有 空兒 嗎？

Dīng Yún: Shénme shìr?
丁　雲： 甚麼 事兒？

Pàlánkǎ: Wǒmen qù chéngwài wánrwanr, hǎo ma?
帕蘭卡： 我們 去 城外 玩兒玩兒， 好 嗎？

Dīng Yún: Hǎo a. Míngtiān jǐdiǎn chūfā?
丁 雲： 好 啊。 明天 几點 出發？

Pàlánkǎ: Qīdiǎnbàn wǒmen kāi chē lái jiē nǐ.
帕蘭卡： 七點半 我們 開 車 來 接 你。

Dīng Yún: Hǎo, zàijiàn!
丁 雲： 好，再見！

第二十四課課文 媽 媽 作 的 點 心

Gǔbō de jiā zài nóngcūn, tā bàba, māma dōu shì nóngmín.
古波 的 家 在 農村， 他 爸爸、媽媽 都 是 農民。

Yìtiān, tā mèimei Ānnà zuò huǒchē lái xuésheng chéng kàn tā.
一天，他 妹妹 安娜 坐 火車 來 學生 城 看 他。

Ānnà bú rènshi Gǔbō de sùshè. Zhè shíhou, pángbiān yǒu yíge
安娜 不 認識 古波 的 宿舍。這 時候， 旁邊 有 一個

xuésheng, tā zhèngzài duànliàn. Ānnà wèn tā: "Qǐngwèn, zhè shì
學生， 他 正在 鍛煉。 安娜 問 他：〝請問， 這 是

liùhào sùshè ma?" Nàge xuésheng huídá: " Bù, zhè shì èrhào.
六號 宿舍 嗎？〞那個 學生 回答：〝不，這是 二號。

Liùhào zài hòubiān, nǐ gēn wǒ lái." Ānnà shuō: " Xièxie nǐ,
六號 在 後邊， 你 跟 我 來。〞 安娜 說：〝謝謝 你，

wǒ qù zhǎo ba."
我 去 找 吧。〞

Ānnà jìn sùshè de shíhou, Gǔbō zhèngzài fùxí Hànyǔ ne.
安娜 進 宿舍 的 時候， 古波 正在 複習 漢語 呢。

Gǔbō shuō:" Shì nǐ a, Ānnà! Wǒ bù zhīdào nǐ jīntiān lái."
古波 說：〝是你 啊， 安娜！ 我 不 知道 你 今天 來。〞

" Nǐ zěnmeyàng, Gǔbō?" Mèimei wèn.
〝你 怎麼樣， 古波？〞妹妹 問。

" Wǒ hěn hǎo. Bàba māma dōu hǎo ma?"
〝我很好。爸爸媽媽都好嗎？〞

"Tāmen dōu hěn hǎo. Kàn, zhè shì māma gěi nǐmen zuò de diǎnxin, nàxiē diǎnxin shì gěi Dīng Yún de."
〝他們都很好。看，這是媽媽給你們作的點心，那些點心是給丁雲的。〞

" Tài hǎo le. Nǐ huí jiā de shíhou xièxie māma."
〝太好了，你回家的時候謝謝媽媽。〞

"Zhè shì hànyǔ shū ma? Wǒ kànkan." Ānnà shuō, "Hànyǔ yídìng hěn nán ba?"
〝這是漢語書嗎？我看看。安娜說，〝漢語一定很難吧？〞

Gǔbō gàosu tā, Hànyǔ yǔfǎ bú tài nán, Hànzì hěn nán. Tā hěn xǐhuan xiě Hànzì. Tā xiànzài hěn máng, měitiān dōu xuéxí shēngcí, niàn kèwén, xiě hànzì, wǎnshang hái zuò liànxí. Měitiān dōu shíyīdiǎn shuì jiào.
古波告訴她，漢語語法不太難，漢字很難。他很喜歡寫漢字。他現在很忙，每天都學習生詞、念課文、寫漢字，晚上還作練習。每天都十一點睡覺。

"Nǐmen de Zhōngguó lǎoshī jiào shénme?" Ānnà wèn.
〝你們的中國老師叫甚麼？〞安娜問。

"Wǒmen de Zhōngguó lǎoshī jiào Wáng Shūwén. Shàng kè de shíhou tā hěn rènzhēn, chángcháng wèn wǒmen dǒng bu dǒng, yǒu mei yǒu wèntí. Xià kè yǐhòu hái gēn wǒmen yìqǐ shuō Hànyǔ. Wǒmen yě chángcháng qù tā nàr wánr."
〝我們的中國老師叫王書文。上課的時候他很認真，常常問我們懂不懂，有沒有問題。下課以後還跟我們一起說漢語。我們也常常去他那兒玩兒。〞

第二十五課課文　他 作 飯 作 得 好 不 好

Pàlánkǎ: Wǒmen lái de tài wǎn le, zài nǎr tíng chē ne?
帕蘭卡： 我們 來 得 太 晚 了，在 哪兒 停 車 呢？

Gǔbō: Zhèr hǎo. Qiánbiān shì tiáo hé, zài zhèr tíng chē ba?
古 波： 這兒 好。 前邊 是 條 河，在 這兒 停 車 吧？

Pàlánkǎ: Hǎo. Wǒ hé Dīng Yún qù yóu yǒng, nǐ zhǔnbèi chī de, hǎo ma?
帕蘭卡： 好。 我 和 丁 雲 去 游 泳，你 準備 吃 的，好 嗎？

Gǔbō: Hǎo ba. Wǒ qù diào yú, qǐng nǐmen hē yú tāng.
古 波： 好 吧。我 去 釣 魚，請 你們 喝 魚 湯。

* * *

Gǔbō: Liǎngwèi xiǎojie, lái ba.
古 波： 兩位 小姐，來 吧。

Pàlánkǎ: Děngyiděng, wǒmen zài xiūxi ne.
帕蘭卡： 等一等， 我們 在 休息 呢。

Gǔbō: Dīng Yún yóu yǒng yóu de zěnmeyàng?
古 波： 丁 雲 游 泳 游 得 怎麼樣？

Pàlánkǎ: Tā yóu de zhēn kuài.
帕蘭卡： 她 游 得 真 快。

Dīng Yún: Nǎli, wǒ yóu de hěn màn. Nǐ yóu de hǎo.
丁 雲： 哪裏，我 游 得 很 慢。你 游 得 好。

Pàlánkǎ: Gǔbō shì wǒ de jiàoliàn, tā jiāo wǒ jiāo de hěn hǎo.
帕蘭卡： 古波 是 我 的 教練，他 教 我 教 得 很 好。

Dīng Yún: Gǔbō zuò fàn zuò de hǎo bu hǎo?
丁 雲： 古波 作 飯 作 得 好 不 好？

Pàlánkǎ: Tā yú tāng zuò de búcuò. Lái, qǐng chī ba!
帕蘭卡： 他 魚 湯 作 得 不錯。 來，請 吃吧！

Gǔbō: Dīng Yún, gěi nǐ miànbāo, huǒtuǐ.
古 波： 丁 雲，給 你 麵包、 火腿。

Pàlánkǎ: Wǒ yào diǎnr nǎilào.
帕蘭卡： 我 要 點兒 奶酪。

Gǔbō: Hǎo. Dīng Yún, zài chī diǎnr ba!
古 波： 好。丁 雲， 再 吃 點兒 吧！

Dīng Yún: Xièxie, wǒ chī de bù shǎo le. Wǒ yào diǎnr tāng.
丁 雲： 謝謝， 我 吃 得 不 少 了。 我 要 點兒 湯。

Gǔbō: Qǐng nǐmen hē —
古 波： 請 你們 喝 —

Pàlánkǎ: Yú tāng?
帕蘭卡： 魚 湯？

Gǔbō: Bù, hē kuàngquánshuǐ.
古 波： 不，喝 礦泉水。

第二十六課課文　我 要 研 究 中 國 文 學

Gǔbō: Wǒmen zǒu ba.
古波： 我們 走 吧。

Pàlánkǎ: Hái zǎo ne, wǒ yào zài gēn Dīng Yún tántan.
帕蘭卡： 還 早 呢，我 要 再 跟 丁 雲 談談。
Dīng Yún, nǐ huì shuō Yīngyǔ hé Fǎyǔ, nǐ yǐhòu
丁 雲，你 會 說 英語 和 法語，你 以後
xiǎng zuò shénme gōngzuò?
想 作 甚麼 工作？

Dīng Yún: Wǒ xiǎng dāng fānyi. Nǐ ne?
丁 雲： 我 想 當 翻譯。你 呢？

Pàlánkǎ: Wǒ yě xiǎng dāng fānyi. Fānyi gōngzuò néng jiā shēn
帕蘭卡： 我 也 想 當 翻譯。翻譯 工作 能 加 深
liǎngguó rénmín de liǎojiě.
兩國 人民 的 了解。

Dīng Yún: Nǐ shuō de zhēn duì. Gǔbō, nǐ xiǎng zuò shénme
丁 雲： 你 說 得 真 對。 古波，你 想 作 甚麼
gōngzuò ne?
工作 呢？

Gǔbō: Wǒ bù xiǎng dāng fānyi. Wǒ yào yánjiū Zhōngguó
古波： 我 不 想 當 翻譯。我 要 研究 中國

wénxué. Zhōngguó yǒu hěn duō yǒumíng de zuòjiā.
文學。 中國 有 很 多 有名 的 作家。

Dīng Yún: Nǐ yào yánjiū nǎwèi zuòjiā?
丁 雲： 你 要 研究 哪位 作家？

Gǔbō: Lǔ Xùn huòzhě Guō Mòruò.
古波： 魯 迅 或者 郭 沫若。

Pàlánkǎ: Jīnnián wǒmen jiù xiǎng qù Zhōngguó xuéxí.
帕蘭卡： 今年 我們 就 想 去 中國 學習。

Dīng Yún: Nǐmen xué de búcuò, yīnggāi qù. Jīnnián néng bu néng qù?
丁 雲： 你們 學 得 不錯， 應該 去。 今年 能 不 能 去？

Pàlánkǎ: Wǒmen liǎ dōu néng qù.
帕蘭卡： 我們 倆 都 能 去。

Dīng Yún: Tài hǎo le, zài nàr nǐmen néng xué de gèng hǎo.
丁 雲： 太 好 了，在 那兒 你們 能 學 得 更 好。

Huí guó yǐhòu, kěyǐ zhǎo yíge lǐxiǎng de gōngzuò.
回 國 以後，可以 找 一個 理想 的 工作。

Gǔbō: Kěshi zhè hěn bù róngyi a!
古波： 可是 這 很 不 容易 啊！

Dīng Yún: "Yǒuzhìzhěshìjìngchéng", zhè shì Zhōngguó de chéngyǔ.
丁 雲： 〝有志者事竟成〞， 這 是 中國 的 成語。

第二十七課課文 電 影 開 始 了 嗎？

(Zài Zhōngguó dàshǐguǎn)
（在 中國 大使館）

Wáng: Nǐmen dōu lái le, qǐng jìn!
王： 你們 都 來 了，請 進！

Bùlǎng: Nín hǎo! Néng cānjiā jīntiān de zhāodàihuì, wǒ fēicháng gāoxìng.
布朗： 您好！ 能 參加 今天 的 招待會， 我 非常 高興。

Gŭbō: Dīng Yún, diànyǐng kāishǐ le ma?
古波： 丁 雲， 電影 開始 了 嗎？

Dīng Yún: Hái méiyou kāishǐ ne. Nǐmen yào hē diǎnr shénme jiǔ?
丁 雲： 還 沒有 開始 呢。 你們 要 喝 點兒 甚麼 酒？

Bùlǎng: Wǒ xiǎng chángchang Zhōngguó de máotáijiǔ.
布朗： 我 想 嘗嘗 中國 的 茅台酒。

Bùlǎng Tàitai: Wǒ bú huì hē jiǔ, yào yìbēi júzishuǐ ba.
布朗太太： 我 不 會 喝 酒，要 一杯 桔子水 吧。

Wáng: Wèi Bùlǎng Xiānsheng hé Bùlǎng Tàitai de jiànkāng gān bēi!
王： 為 布朗 先生 和 布朗 太太 的 健康 乾 杯！

Bùlǎng: Xièxie, wèi wǒmen de yǒuyì gān bēi!
布朗： 謝謝， 為 我們 的 友誼 乾 杯！

Dīng Yún: Pàlánkǎ, máotáijiǔ nǐ hē le méiyou?
丁 雲： 帕蘭卡，茅台酒 你 喝 了 沒有？

Pàlánkǎ: Méiyou. Wǒ hē le yìbēi Zhōngguó pútaojiǔ.
帕蘭卡： 沒有。 我 喝了 一杯 中國 葡萄酒。

Dīng Yún: Qǐng nǐmen chángchang Zhōngguó cài.
丁 雲： 請 你們 嘗嘗 中國 菜。

Tàitai: Xièxie, wǒ chī le. Fēicháng hǎo.
太太： 謝謝， 我 吃 了。 非常 好。

Gŭbō: Kuàizi wǒ hái yòng de bù hǎo, wǒ xiǎng zài shìyishi.
古波： 筷子 我 還 用 得 不 好，我 想 再 試一試。

* * *

Wáng: Wǒ gěi nǐmen jièshaojièshao: Zhè shì dàshǐguǎn de wénhuà
王： 我 給 你們 介紹介紹： 這 是 大使館 的 文化

cānzàn Lǐ Xiānsheng hé fūren, zhè shì Bùlǎng Xiānsheng
參贊 李 先生 和 夫人，這 是 布朗 先生

hé Bùlǎng Tàitai.
和 布朗 太太。

Bùlǎng: Rènshi nǐmen, wǒ hěn gāoxìng.
布朗： 認識 你們，我 很 高興。

Cānzàn: Huānyíng, huānyíng.
參贊： 歡迎，　歡迎。

Wáng: Zhè liǎngwèi shì Zhōngwén xì de xuésheng, Gǔbō hé Pàlánkǎ.
王： 這　兩位　是　中文　系 的 學生，　古波 和　帕蘭卡。

Tāmen jīnnián jiǔyuè jiù yào qù Zhōngguó xuéxí.
他們　今年 九月　就 要 去　中國　學習。

Cānzàn: Tài hǎo le, wǒmen yòu rènshi le liǎngwèi niánqīng de péngyou.
參贊： 太 好 了，我們　又 認識 了 兩位　年輕　的 朋友。

Fūren: Qǐng dàjiā dào lóushàng kàn diànyǐng ba.
夫人： 請　大家 到　樓上　看　電影　吧。

第二十八課課文　我 去 看 足 球 賽 了

Pàlánkǎ: Gǔbō, zuótiān shàngwǔ wǒ gěi nǐ dǎ diànhuà le,
帕蘭卡： 古波，昨天　上午　我 給 你 打 電話　了，

nǐ bú zài. Nǐ qù nǎr le?
你 不 在。你　去 哪兒了？

Gǔbō: Wǒ qù Zhōngguó dàshǐguǎn bàn qiānzhèng le.
古波： 我 去　中國　大使館　辦　簽證　了。

Pàlánkǎ: Xiàwǔ ne? Nǐ yòu bú zài.
帕蘭卡： 下午　呢？你　又 不 在。

Gǔbō: Wǒ chī le wǔfàn jiù qù kàn zúqiú sài le.
古波： 我　吃了　午飯 就　去 看　足球 賽 了。

Pàlánkǎ: Shéi gēn shéi sài?
帕蘭卡： 誰　跟　誰 賽？

Gǔbō: Dàxuéshēng duì gēn yínháng duì sài.
古波： 大學生　隊 跟　銀行　隊 賽。

Pàlánkǎ: Dàxuéshēng duì yíng tāmen le ma?
帕蘭卡： 大學生　隊　贏 他們　了　嗎？

Gǔbō: Méiyou, dàxuéshēng duì shū le, yī bǐ èr. Cáipàn bù gōngping.
古波： 沒有，　大學生　隊 輸了，一比二。 裁判 不 公平。

Pàlánkǎ: Nǐ zǒng shuō cáipàn bù gōngping.
帕蘭卡： 你 總　説　裁判 不 公平。

Gǔbō: Nǐ méi qù kàn, zuótiān dàxuéshēng duì tī de hěn hǎo.
古波： 你 沒 去 看，昨天 大學生 隊 踢 得 很 好。

Zhēn qì rén.
真 氣 人。

Pàlánkǎ: Hǎo le, wǒ wèn nǐ, nǐ de xíngli zhǔnbèi de zěnmeyàng?
帕蘭卡： 好了，我 問 你，你的行李 準備 得 怎麼樣？

Gǔbō: Wǒ zhèng zhěnglǐ xiāngzi ne. Wǒ hái chà yìdǐng màozi.
古波： 我 正 整理 箱子 呢。 我 還 差 一頂 帽子。

Nǐ ne?
你 呢？

Pàlánkǎ: Wǒ xiǎng mǎi yìshuāng bīngxié. Běijīng dōngtiān kěyǐ
帕蘭卡： 我 想 買 一雙 冰鞋。 北京 冬天 可以

huá bīng.
滑 冰。

Gǔbō: Wǒ sòng nǐ yìshuāng bīngxié ba.
古波： 我 送 你 一雙 冰鞋 吧。

Pàlánkǎ: Fēicháng gǎnxiè. Wǒ gěi nǐ mǎi màozi, hǎo ma?
帕蘭卡： 非常 感謝。 我 給 你 買 帽子， 好 嗎？

Gǔbō: Wǒ yě yào xièxie nǐ. Míngtiān chī le zǎofàn wǒmen
古波： 我 也 要 謝謝 你。明天 吃 了 早飯 我們

jiù qù shāngdiàn.
就 去 商店。

第二十九課課文 飛 機 就 要 起 飛 了

(Zài jīchǎng)
（在 機場）

Gǔbō: Nǐ kàn, tóngxuémen dōu lái le, Wáng Lǎoshī hé Dīng Yún
古波： 你 看，同學們 都 來了，王 老師 和 丁 雲

yě lái le.
也 來 了。

Pàlánkǎ: Dīng Yún, wǒmen kuài yào fēnbié le, wǒ zhēn bú yuànyì
帕蘭卡： 丁 雲， 我們 快 要 分別 了，我 真 不 願意

líkāi nǐ.
離開你。

Dīng Yún: Pàlánkǎ, wǒ yě bú yuànyì líkāi nǐ.
丁　雲：帕蘭卡，我 也 不 願意 離開 你。

Wǒ xiǎng wǒmen hěn kuài huì zài Zhōngguó jiàn miàn.
我 想 我們 很 快 會 在 中國 見 面。

Gǔbō: Wáng Lǎoshī, wǒmen fēicháng gǎnxiè nín.
古波：王 老師， 我們 非常 感謝 您。

Bùlǎng: Wǒ tàitai hé wǒ yě yào xièxie nín. Nín gōngzuò fēicháng
布朗：我 太太 和 我 也 要 謝謝 您。您 工作 非常

rènzhēn, jiāo de hěn hǎo, suǒyi tāmen jìnbù hěn kuài.
認真， 教 得 很 好，所以 他們 進步 很 快。

Wáng: Nǎlǐ, zhè shì wǒ yīnggāi zuò de. Tāmen xuéxí dōu hěn
王：哪里，這 是 我 應該 作 的。他們 學習 都 很

nǔlì, suǒyǐ néng xué de hěn hǎo.
努力，所以能 學 得 很 好。

Pàlánkǎ: Bàba yào gěi wǒmen zhàoxiàng le.
帕蘭卡：爸爸 要 給 我們 照像 了。

Bùlǎng: Qǐng dàjiā zhàn de jǐn yìdiǎnr! Hǎo. Gǔbō,
布朗：請 大家 站 得 緊 一點兒！好。古波，

nǐmen zhǔnbeizhǔnbei jiù shàng fēijī ba.
你們 準備準備 就 上 飛機 吧。

Tàitai: Pàlánkǎ, nǐmen yào zhùyì shēntǐ.
太太：帕蘭卡，你們 要 注意 身體。

Pàlánkǎ: Māma nín fàng xīn, wǒmen shēntǐ dōu hěn hǎo.
帕蘭卡：媽媽 您 放 心，我們 身體 都 很 好。

Tàitai: Nǐmen dào le Běijīng jiù gěi wǒ lái xìn. Bié wàng le,
太太：你們 到 了 北京 就 給 我 來 信。別 忘 了，

yídìng yào lái xìn.
一定 要 來 信。

Bùlǎng: Hǎo le, bié nánguò le. Míngnián wǒmen qù Zhōngguó kàn tāmen.
布朗：好 了，別 難過了。明年 我們 去 中國 看 他們。

Gǔbō: Nǐmen míngnián shénme shíhou qù Běijīng? Wǒmen
古波： 你們 明年 甚麼 時候 去 北京？ 我們

yídìng dào jīchǎng jiē nǐmen.
一定 到 機場 接 你們。

Bùlǎng: Míngnián xiàtiān huòzhě qiūtiān qù. Fēijī jiù yào
布朗： 明年 夏天 或者 秋天 去。 飛機 就 要

qǐfēi le, nǐmen kuài zǒu ba.
起飛 了，你們 快 走 吧。

Wáng: Zhù nǐmen shēntǐ hǎo, xuéxí hǎo!
王： 祝 你們 身體 好，學習 好！

Dīng Yún: Zhù nǐmen yílùpíng'ān!
丁 雲： 祝 你們 一路平安！

Pàlánkǎ, Gǔbō: Xièxie dàjiā. Zàijiàn!
帕蘭卡、古波： 謝謝 大家。 再見！

第三十課課文 布 朗 太 太 笑 了

Pàlánkǎ zǒu le, Bùlǎng Tàitai xīnli hěn nánguò. Tā qǐng Dīng Yún
帕蘭卡 走 了，布朗 太太 心裏 很 難過。 她 請 丁 雲

zuò tā de chē, tā yào sòng Dīng Yún huí xuésheng sùshè.
坐 她 的 車，她 要 送 丁 雲 回 學生 宿舍。

Zài chēshang, Dīng Yún shuō: " Pàlánkǎ hěn xiǎng qù Zhōngguó
在 車上， 丁 雲 說：〝帕蘭卡很 想 去 中國

xuéxí, tā jīntiān wǎnshang jiù yào dào Běijīng le, wǒ xiǎng tā xiànzài
學習，她 今天 晚上 就 要 到 北京 了，我 想 她 現在

yídìng hěn gāoxìng."
一定 很 高興。〞

Bùlǎng Xiānsheng shuō: " Nǚ'ér hěn gāoxìng de shíhou, māma
布朗 先生 說：〝女兒 很 高興 的 時候，媽媽

xīnli hěn nánguò."
心裏 很 難過。〞

Bùlǎng Tàitai wèn Dīng Yún: " Qùnián nǐ lái wǒmen guójiā de
布朗 太太 問 丁 雲：〝去年 你 來 我們 國家 的

shíhou, nǐ māma yuànyì nǐ líkāi tā ma?"
時候，你媽媽 願意 你 離開 她 嗎？〃

Dīng Yún gàosu Bùlǎng Tàitai, tā māma kāishǐ hěn gāoxìng,
丁 雲 告訴 布朗 太太，她 媽媽 開始 很 高興，

gěi tā mǎi le hěn duō dōngxi. Māma yào tā zhùyì shēntǐ, nǔlì xuéxí,
給 她 買 了 很 多 東西。 媽媽 要 她 注意 身體，努力 學習，

bú yào xiǎng jiā. Tā zǒu de nà tiān, kuài shàng fēijī le, tā shuō
不 要 想 家。她 走 的 那 天，快 上 飛機 了， 她 說

"zàijiàn", māma jiù kū le.
〝再見〞，媽媽 就 哭 了。

"Shì a!" Bùlǎng Tàitai shuō. Tā yòu wèn: " Zhèr lí Běijīng
〝是啊！〞布朗 太太 說。 她 又 問：〝這兒 離 北京

hěn yuǎn, nǐ māma fàngxīn ma?"
很 遠， 你 媽媽 放心 嗎？〞

Dīng Yún shuō: "Wǒ chángcháng gěi māma xiě xìn, gàosù tā
丁 雲 說："我 常常 給 媽媽 寫 信，告訴 她

zhèr de lǎoshī hé tóngxué dōu hěn rèqíng, wǒ zài zhèr guò de hěn hǎo.
這兒 的 老師 和 同學 都 很 熱情，我 在 這兒 過 得 很 好。

Wǒ hái gàosu māma, Pàlánkǎ shì wǒ de hǎo péngyou, tā jiù xiàng wǒ
我 還 告訴 媽媽， 帕蘭卡 是 我 的 好 朋友， 她 就 像 我

de mèimei, tā de jiā jiù xiàng wǒ zìjǐ de jiā. Suǒyǐ māma xiànzài hěn
的 妹妹，她 的 家 就 像 我 自己 的 家。所以 媽媽 現在 很

fàngxīn. Zuótiān wǒ yòu xiě xìn gàosu tāmen, Pàlánkǎ kuài yào qù Zhōngguó
放心。 昨天 我 又 寫 信 告訴 他們，帕蘭卡 快 要 去 中國

xuéxí le, tā dào le Běijīng jiù yào qù kànkan māma." Bùlǎng Xiānsheng
學習 了，她 到 了 北京 就 要 去 看看 媽媽。〞 布朗 先生

shuō: "Pàlánkǎ rènshi le yíge Zhōngguó jiějie, tā dào Běijīng yǐhòu,
說：〝帕蘭卡 認識 了 一個 中國 姐姐，她 到 北京 以後，

yòu yào rènshi yíwèi Zhōngguó māma." Bùlǎng Tàitai xiào le.
又 要 認識 一位 中國 媽媽。〞布朗 太太 笑 了。

第三十一課課文　我們學了兩年的中文了

古波：　請問，您是中國人嗎？

老華僑：　是啊，我是華僑，從美國來，你們中國話說得不錯，
學了幾年的中文了？

古波：　哪裏，還差得遠呢。我們學了兩年中文了。

帕蘭卡：　您在美國很長時間了吧？

老華僑：　我在美國已經四十多年了。

古波：　您常回中國嗎？

老華僑：　不，這是第二次。一九六五年我第一次回國，
參觀了工廠、農村和很多學校，在上海住了三個多月。

帕蘭卡：　您在美國作甚麼工作？

老華僑：　在大學工作。我教書已經教了三十多年了。

古波：　您家裏還有人在北京嗎？

老華僑：　有。我弟弟、妹妹都在北京。 他們正在為實現四個
現代化努力工作。我這次回國看看，希望能為社會
主義建設作一點事兒。

帕蘭卡：　古波，還有五分鐘就要到北京了。

古波：　再見吧，老先生。

老華僑：　再見，祝你們學習好，身體好。

帕蘭卡：　謝謝！

（在首都國際機場）

張華光：　請問，你是古波同學嗎？

古波：　對，我叫古波，她叫帕蘭卡。我們要去北京語言
學院學習。

張華光：　太好了！我是北京語言學院的學生代表，我叫張華光。這位是趙同志。

趙同志：　歡迎你們！路上辛苦了，你們坐了多長時間的飛機？

帕蘭卡：　坐了十幾個小時。北京的天氣真好。

趙同志：　是啊，今天天氣不錯。手續辦了嗎？

古波：　手續都辦了。

趙同志：　好，請大家上車吧。

第三十二課課文　　你最近透視過沒有

古波：　小張，醫務所在哪兒？

張華光：　你去看病嗎？

古波：　不，我去檢查身體。我還沒去過醫務所呢。

張華光：　跟我走吧。來北京一個多星期了，你們去過哪些地方了？

古波：　去過長城和北海。

張華光：　看過什麼電影嗎？

古波：　在電視裏看過幾次電影。

張華光：　今天晚上學校有電影，你去嗎？

古波：　甚麼電影？

張華光：　《大鬧天宮》。這個電影真不錯，我已經看過兩遍了。

古波：　還想看第三遍嗎？今天晚上我們一起去吧。

張華光：　好。醫務所到了，你在那兒拿一張表，先到內科檢查。

*　　*　　*

古波：　大夫，您好！

大夫：　你好，請坐。你第一次來中國嗎？

古波：　是啊。也是第一次來醫務所。

大夫：　你以前得過甚麼病？

古波：　沒有。一 對了，我小時候得過肺炎，病了兩個多星期。

大夫：　聽聽心臟，量一下兒血壓吧。…

古波：　大夫，我的心臟和血壓都正常嗎？

大夫：　都很正常。你最近透視過沒有？

古波：　去年二月透視過一次。

大夫：　時間太長了。請到對面房間透視一下兒吧。

古波：　透視以後就可以走了嗎？

大夫：　不，還要檢查一下兒眼睛、鼻子和耳朵。

古波：　我想這些都沒有問題。

大夫：　我也希望這樣。

古波：　謝謝。我聽過這樣的話：爸爸媽媽給我生命，老師給我知識，大夫給我健康。

大夫：　這話很有意思。可是我希望你的健康不是大夫給的，要自己注意鍛煉。祝你健康，再見！

第三十三課課文　現在下雨了

帕蘭卡：　四點多了，李老師不來了吧？

古波：　聽，有人敲門，李老師來了。

李老師：　古波在嗎？

古波：　在，請進。

李老師：　啊，帕蘭卡也在這兒。你們好！

帕蘭卡：　您好，請坐。李老師，請您喝杯咖啡吧？

李老師：　謝謝。今天天氣很好，你們沒到公園玩兒玩兒嗎？

古波：　上午去頤和園了。

李老師：　香山去過嗎？

帕蘭卡：　還沒去過。那兒怎麼樣？

李老師：　香山的紅葉很漂亮。現在是秋天了，樹上的葉子都紅了，可以看紅葉了。

古波：　我們一定去。以前有人告訴我，北京的夏天很熱，到北京以後，我覺得不太熱。

李老師：　這幾年天氣不熱。你知道嗎？北京的秋天天氣最好，可是今年秋天也常常下雨。你們看，今天上午是晴天，現在下雨了。

古波：　北京冬天冷不冷？

李老師：　冬天很冷，常常刮風、下雪。

帕蘭卡：　在中國冬天有甚麼花兒？

李老師：　很多地方有梅花。在大風大雪的天氣，梅花不怕風，不怕雪，開得很好，所以大家都喜歡梅花。從古時候到今天，文學家為梅花寫了不少詩。

古波：　您教我們一首，好嗎？

李老師：　這樣的詩很多。我給你們唸一首吧，是陳毅的

《紅梅》：　隆冬到來時，百花跡已絕。
紅梅不屈服，樹樹立風雪。

帕蘭卡：　這首詩真好，請您再介紹一首。

李老師：　時間不早了，雨也停了，我們以後再介紹吧。古波，這是你要的那本語法書。

古波：　謝謝您。您再坐坐吧。

李老師：　不坐了，我還有點事兒，再見！

帕蘭卡：　希望您常來，再見！

第三十四課課文　圖片上寫 着〝怎樣寫信封？〞

下了一上午的雨，下午天晴了。

帕蘭卡跟丁云分別的時候，丁云跟她說過：到北京以後一定要去家裏看看。今天，她給丁云的媽媽寫了一封信，問她們甚麼時間有空兒，她想去看他們。古波也要給南京的朋友寄一封信，他們一起去郵局。

六點多了，郵局的門還開 着呢。郵局裏人很多，有的坐 着寫信，有的等 着寄東西。他們到了一個窗口前邊。　那兒掛着一個牌子，牌子上寫着〝郵票・掛號〞；櫃台裏放着很多漂亮的郵票和明信片。　帕蘭卡跟營業員說：〝同志，我想買幾張明信片。〞營業員熱情地回答：〝有，這兒有介紹北京的。 請看， 天安門、北海、頤和園、香山……。我想您一定很喜歡。〞帕蘭卡笑着說：〝對，就要這些。我想讓家裏人也看看北京。〞

古波拿着他的信跟營業員說：〝我要寄航空掛號信。營業員看了看信封說：〝寄本市的信沒有航空的。〞古波大聲地說：〝不，這不是本市的，是寄南京的。〞營業員又看了看古波的信封，她笑了; 帕蘭卡一看，也笑了。她們為甚麼笑呢？古波的信封，上邊寫　着他自己的地址和姓名，下邊寫　着收信人的地址、姓名。營業員指　着牆上的圖片說：〝中國的信封應該這樣寫。〞古波一看，圖片上寫 着：〝怎樣寫信封？〞……

第三十五課課文　　談 學 習

時間過得真快，古波和帕蘭卡到北京快一個月了。帕蘭卡怕媽媽不放心，已經給家裏寫過三次信，還寄了一些照片。媽媽也給她來過兩封信。

到北京語言學院的第三天，他們就參加了一次考試。 這次考試，有的同學考得非常好，有的差一點兒。他們倆的成績都不錯。李老師說，他們先在語言學院學習一學期漢語，以後再到北京大學學習專業。古波覺得自己的口語不太好，這半年要更多地練習聽和說。現在，他每天下午都跟他的好朋友張華光說一個小時的漢語。小張是外語系英語專業的學生，他在這兒已經學了一年多了。他進步很快，現在可以跟古波用英語談話了。今天，他問古波：〝你在你們國家學習中文的時候，怎麼樣練習口語呢？〞古波說：〝來中國以前，我說中國話的機會也很少。有一個中國留學生叫丁雲，她非常熱情地幫助我們。上課的時候，中國老師總是讓我們多說、多念。可是你知道，每學期我們上課的時間不太多。夏天到了放暑假; 冬天來了放寒 假。在假期裏 我沒有時間複習。小張一聽，覺得很奇怪：〝你們的假期很長，為甚麼不能複習複習學過的東西呢？〞古波笑 着回答：〝你沒到過我們國家，不了解那兒的情況。我們的暑假很長，可是我常常利用假期工作，掙點兒錢，開學以後用。現在好了，在這兒說漢語的機會多了，以後我們互相幫助吧。〞

古波和小張正在宿舍里談着話，帕蘭卡來了。她 着急地問：〝已經六點多了，你們還坐 着說話，不吃飯了嗎？〞古波一看錶，啊，真太晚了。他們一起去食堂吃飯。

APPENDIX B

The following is the key to the exercises in Lessons 21-35, PCR.

第二十一課

4. (1) 介紹介紹 (2) 用用 (3) 找找 (4) 休息休息 (5) 問問
   (6) 幫助幫助

第二十二課

2. (1) 桌子上邊有一杯茶。 桌子上邊是一杯茶。
   (2) 書店和咖啡館中間有一個銀行。 書店和咖啡館中間是銀行。
   (3) 廚房外邊有一個餐廳。 廚房外邊是餐廳。
   (4) 房子前邊有一個花園。 房子前邊是花園。
   (5) 學院左邊有一個圖書館。 學院左邊是圖書館。
   (6) 書房旁邊有一個客廳。 書房旁邊是客廳。
3. 前邊，裏邊，中間，右邊，旁邊，左邊，對面，左邊，
   右邊，中間

第二十三課

5. (1) 休息的時候 (2) 參觀工廠的人 (3) 媽媽給她的襯衫
   (4) 我買的那本書 (5) 他認識的新朋友
6. (1) 我去的時候，他正看電視呢。
   (2) 他們出發的時候，我正起床呢。
   (3) 留學生是在國外學習的學生。
   (4) 在咖啡館工作的人叫服務員。
   (5) 他買衣服的那個商店不太大。
   (6) 教你們漢語的老師是誰？

第二十四課

1. 六個班，十二個同學， 十瓶（杯）啤酒， 三杯咖啡 ，
六十二個工人，八十五個農民，四個代表團，七個問題，
四張照片，十一張票，五個房間，八件襯衫，三十二個字，
二十六個詞，一個圖書館，一束花兒，二十二張桌子，
三條裙子，九個工廠，十五個服務員

4. (1) 的妹妹，十八，從
(2) 在，忙，回，今天來
(3) 進宿舍的，複習，寫，念，作
(4) 懂，認識，難，難
(5) 很好，漢語，認真，下課，幫助，喜歡

5. (1) 帕蘭卡星期五去古波宿舍。
(2) 一九七九年九月四號他去中國。
(3) 我們班有十四個學生。
(4) 那天我跟他一起去看電影。
(5) 左邊的那本畫報是我的。
(6) 我很喜歡這五個歌兒。
(7) 他複習課文的時候，我正鍛煉呢。
(8) 今天他高興不高興？
(9) 這些生詞很難。
(10) 他寫漢字寫得很好。
(11) 我回答老師問的問題。
(12) 他住125號房間。
(13) 我們請他介紹介紹漢語語法。
(14) 他是一個很認真的老師。
(15) 晚上我去看我的一個朋友。
(16) 她的那件襯衫很漂亮。

第二十五課

2. (1) 得很高興 (2) 得很認真 (3) 説得很好
(4) 游得很快 (5) 學得不太好 (6) 問得很多

3. (1) A: 他寫漢字寫得怎麼樣？
(2) A: 你開車開得快不快？
(3) A: 他跳舞跳得好嗎？
(4) A: 那個學生來得晚不晚？
(5) B: 謝謝，我吃得不少了。

第二十六課

4. 要，想，能不能，想，能，應該，可以，可以，會

5. (1) 他想當大夫。 (2) 你要不要買京劇票？
(3) 他很會釣魚。 (4) 閲覽室裏不能唱歌。
(5) 你應該每天鍛煉。 (6) 他能教你英語。
(7) 今天晚上你能不能看電視？ (8) 你可以了解得更多。
(9) 我想研究中國的成語。

第二十七課

6. (1) 又 (2) 再 (3) 又 (4) 再 (5) 再 (6) 又

第二十八課

3. (1) B: 我去看比利了。
B: 他（在宿舍）整理箱子了。
(2) A: 星期日你們去哪兒玩兒了？
B: 她沒有去。
(3) B: 我參觀農村了。
B: 我們訪問農民的家了。
(4) B: 我接（電話）了。

A: 誰給你打電話了？

(5) B: 我去商店了。

A: 你在商店買甚麼了 ？

(6) A: 你給他們買足球票了沒有 ？

A: 他們去不去看足球賽?

第二十九課

4. (1) B: 別忘了 (2) B: 別難過了 (3) B: 別跳了

(4) B: 別找了 (5) B: 別玩兒了

5. (1) 你爸爸媽媽身體好嗎 ？ (2) 那個裁判工作怎麼樣 ？

(3) 我們學院留學生不多。 (4) 她家廚房很小， 餐廳很大。

(5) 這個商店襯衫好不好？

第三十課

3. (1) 昨天我參加了比賽了。 你參加沒參加 ？

(2) 晚上我作了練習就聽音樂。 你聽不聽？

(3) 我辦了簽證了。 你辦沒辦 ？

(4) 昨天我在我同學那兒看了電視。 你看沒看 ？

(5) 晚上我作了兩個菜 。 你作沒作？

(6) 星期天我跟我朋友一起聽了唱片 。 你聽沒聽 ？

5. (1) 給 (2) 跟 (3) 從 (4) 給 (5) 離 (6) 給 (7) 為 (8) 給

6. (1) 明天你朋友能去參加舞會嗎?

(2) 別等了， 他今天不會來 。

(3) 大夫說你要注意身體 。

(4) 那個問題他研究得怎麼樣？

(5) 他告訴我他快要離開這兒了。

(6) 你願意幫助我學習法語嗎 ？

7. (1) +　(2) −　(3) −　(4) +　(5) −　(6) +　(7) −　(8) −　(9) −　(10) +

8. (1) 晚上他寫了一封信　。（晚上他寫信了　。）

(2) 明天我下了課就去看電影 。

(3) 昨天我去他家的時候，他正看電視呢 。

(4) 去年我常常參加足球比賽 。

(5) 冬天我沒有滑冰 。

(6) 他很早地起床了。

(7) 我想看中國電影。

(8) 他們讓我唱了一個中國民歌　。

(9) 代表團坐飛機去中國了。

(10) 有時候我跟他一起釣魚 。

(11) 老師問了我一個問題 。

(12) 同學們都試了試中國筷子 。

第三十一課

2. (1) 參觀了三個半小時　　(2) 教了四十多年了

(3) 開了半個小時　　(4) 寫了兩年多了

(5) 在北京（住）兩年　　(6) 睡八個半小時

5. (1) 去年秋天那個留學生第一次回國 。

(2) 他下午兩點開始參觀，參觀了兩個小時 。

(3) 我們每星期學習六天，休息一天 。

(4) 晚上他有時候看半個小時的電視，有時候聽一刻多鐘的新聞 。

(5) 這本語法書他已經翻譯了兩個多月了。

(6) 今年夏天我沒有在上海住很長時間，我在那兒住了幾天。

(7) 中國留學生為實現四個現代化努力學習。

第三十二課

3. ⑴ 遍 ⑵ 次 ⑶ 遍 ⑷ 次 ⑸ 下兒 ⑹ 下兒 ⑺ 次，次

第三十三課

4. ⑴ 我離開家的時候天氣很好，現在刮風了，快要下雨了。
⑵ 以前有人告訴我中國的梅花很多，也很好看。
⑶ 天氣熱了，可以去游泳了。你去嗎？
⑷ 今天下午我很忙，有一個朋友要來看我。
⑸ 最近天天都刮風。
⑹ 他不怕冷，很怕熱。
⑺ 他以前當翻譯，現在當老師了。
⑻ 我覺得這兒的夏天最好。
⑼ 這本書我再看一星期，可以嗎？
⑽ 他病了，從星期一到今天沒有來上課。

第三十四課

2. ⑴ 挂着 ⑵ 放着 ⑶ 開着 ⑷ 拿着
⑸ 穿着 ⑹ 站着 ⑺ 指着 ⑻ 開着

3. ⑴ 有的人，有的人 ⑵ 有的，有的
⑶ 有的同學 ⑷ 有時候，有時候

4. ⑴ 我去郵局的時候，那位營業員總是熱情地幫助我。
⑵ 孩子哭着説：“我不去學校。”
⑶ 你知道怎麼樣用筷子嗎？
⑷ 銀行的櫃台前邊站着很多人。
⑸ 大夫仔細地檢查了他的身體以後笑着説：“你的心臟，血壓都很正常。”
⑹ 他一聽，覺得這個歌兒非常好。
⑺ 你看，這個漢字應該這樣寫。

(8) 你為甚麼喜歡梅花 ?

第三十五課

1. 天:　今天，昨天，明天，春天，夏天，秋天，冬天，晴天

　學:　學生，留學生，同學，學習，大學，學院，學校

　假:　暑假，寒假，放假，假期

　文:　中文，英文，法文，課文，文化，文學

　語:　漢語，英語，法語，外語，口語，語法，成語，語言

　飯:　吃飯，早飯，午飯，晚飯

2. (1) 熱情地　(2) 認真地　(3) 着急地

　(4) 高興地　(5) 大聲地　(6) 更多地

3. (1) 就　(2) 再　(3) 還　(4) 再　(5) 還

　(6) 再　(7) 還　(8) 又　(9) 還　(10) 還

4. (1) 他今天穿着一雙新鞋。

　(2) 這位營業員以前在那個郵局工作過。

　(3) 學了這首詩你可以了解一點兒這位作家的情況。

　(4) 大夫正給他看病呢。

　(5) 梅花快要開了。

　(6) 誰在敲門呢 ?

　(7) 刮風了，快要下雨了。

　(8) 你拿過這兒的圖片嗎 ?

　(9) 他利用假期工作，掙了一些錢。

　(10) 別站着了，請坐吧。

5. 着，着，着，着，

　了，了，着，過，着，過，着，了

　了，了，了，了

6. (1) 他病了很長時間了。

(2) 這個問題應該這樣回答。

(3) 小張在河邊釣着魚呢 。

(4) 那個電影我看了兩次 。

(5) 她在前邊站 着。

(6) 他以前到英國學過英文。

(7) 我以前不會照像，現在會照像了。

(8) 古波要努力（地）學習中文。